Dr. Shintani's HawaiiDiet™ Cookbook

by

Terry T. Shintani, M.D., J.D., M.P.H.

HEALTH FOUNDATION PRESS
P. O. Box 37337
Honolulu, Hawaii 96837

Editor's Note: In the spelling of Hawaiian words, macrons have been omitted and glottal stop marks have been represented as apostrophes because these punctuation marks are not available in the font used in this book.

Cover art and graphics by Carol Devenot

ISBN 0-9636117-9-8

1st Printing, October, 1997

10 9 8 7 6 5 4 3

Printed in North America.

Dedication

This book is dedicated to our almighty Father, the "Great Physician" who is the source of all healing.

&

Contents

x

∞

Preface
by the Honorable Benjamin J. Cayetano

As Governor of the State of Hawaii, and as a participant of the 21-day traditional HawaiiDiet™ in January, 1997, I would like to share with you my truly remarkable results.

The HawaiiDiet™ started me on the right path to a healthier lifestyle. By staying with a traditional eating pattern of the ancient Hawaiian people combined with other ethnic foods of our multicultural state, my weight loss and lower levels of blood sugar and cholesterol have been remarkable.

When I started, my weight was 198 pounds, my cholesterol level was a high 234 mg/dl, and my triglyceride level *(blood fat)* was up to an abnormal 617 mg/dl. Now I weigh 12 pounds less, my cholesterol level is down to 162 mg/dl, and my triglyceride level is normal at 83 mg/dl.

I feel healthier and more energetic. I have actually reduced my need for high blood pressure medication.

Others of my staff also participated in the HawaiiDiet™ Program:

- My Chief of Staff started the diet with a blood pressure reading of 152/85 while on medication. Halfway through the diet, he was taken off his blood pressure medication. His blood pressure reading on the last day was 122/86 while off medication. He also lost 7-3/4 pounds and reduced his cholesterol level from 177 mg/dl to 125 mg/dl.

- Our Human Services Director not only lost 9 pounds, she is now out of the high risk category, having reduced her cholesterol level from 245 mg/dl to 161 mg/dl.

- My Executive Assistant's weight loss is over 15-1/2 pounds, and he reduced his cholesterol level from 218 mg/dl to 149 mg/dl.

These results show what can be done by following the HawaiiDiet™. The 21-day Hawaii Health Program has taught me the importance of a low-fat diet. It's a simple prevention measure that works and reduces the cost of medical health care.

I urge everyone interested in a healthier diet and lifestyle to try the HawaiiDiet™.

Honorable Benjamin J. Cayetano
Governor of the State of Hawaii
January 28, 1997

ℰ

A Word of Gratitude

In January of 1997, a crowd decked out in Polynesian elegance mixed on the *lanai* at Washington Place, the home of Hawaii's Governor, Ben Cayetano. We were there for a *pa'ina*, a celebration of the conclusion of a three-week diet and health program conducted by Dr. Shintani and the Hawaii Health Foundation. Gathered were many program participants, staff and volunteers and their families, and an array of prominent locals. We listened as the Governor shared his remarkable success on the program; we ate healthy, delicious food from the program; and we enjoyed the music of Auntie Genoa Keawe.

On the wave of the Governor's Diet have come HawaiiDiet™ programs at Kamehameha Schools, Halawa Housing, Papakolea Homestead, and more *pa'ina*, humbler but all unforgettable. Lucky me, a *malihini*, a newcomer, to have memories of an a capella hymn so beautifully sung at Halawa, *Hawaii Aloha* sweetly sung at Kamehameha, a *Papakolea* hula so warmly danced and sung, complete with a view of Punchbowl and an off-key kid, that I wished they would never stop. And, always, testimony from the participants that their weights had gone down, that their blood pressure, their asthma, their diabetic conditions had improved. Always, their honest gratitude to Dr. Shintani and the Hawaii Health Foundation for helping replace fear with hope, fear for their health with hope for their lives. Lucky me, to be treated to a multi-ethnic variety of foods that would delight any mainlander's palate. Lucky me, to be shown by example again and again that Hawaiian values like *lokahi*, *malama*, and *aloha* are not abstractions but are like a big recipe for well-being, for *pono*.

Thank you, Dr. Shintani, for voicing the riches of Hawaiian wisdom and for all the *'ono* food. And, thank you and Diane, your hard-working Administrator, and everyone else associated with the programs for the *ho'okipa*, the hospitality, shown a newcomer to these beautiful islands.

– David McDonald, Assistant Editor

☙

Acknowledgments

Producing this book required a great deal of effort and thought from many people, spanning a period of several years.

The fundamentals of this book come from my work in private practice. The diet utilizes a variety of plant-based foods from various traditional cultures in order to induce weight loss, improve health, and reduce the need for medication in my patients. Much of this background research appears in my original work with the *Eat More, Weigh Less®Diet,* which I first presented in 1986 and which has been refined over the intervening years. In addition, it incorporates new research that we have conducted, which demonstrates the effectiveness of traditional diet on the reversal of obesity and chronic disease.

The Waianae Diet, which was first implemented in 1989, and for which planning began in mid-1987 at the Waianae Coast Comprehensive Health Center *(WCCHC)* also provided some material for this book.

This information has been further developed through the HawaiiDiet™ Study *(which compared the health effects of traditional Hawaii/Pacific diet with that of a Mediterranean diet)* and the HawaiiDiet™ Program, which has been popularly called "The Governor's Diet" because of the participation of Hawaii's Governor, the Honorable Benjamin J. Cayetano.

It would be impossible to recognize here every person who influenced this book or participated in some way in its production. However, I would like to give special thanks to the following organizations and individuals:

- The Waianae Coast Comprehensive Health Center, their owners, the Waianae Coast Community, and their staff, especially Helen Kanawaliwali O'Connor and Sheila Beckham, M.P.H., R.D., who helped to develop the original Waianae Diet Program *(WDP)*.

- Claire Hughes, M.S., R.D., whom I consider one of the cofounders of the WDP, and Kekuni Blaisdell, M.D., one of my professors and mentors.

- The Office of Hawaiian Affairs *(OHA)*, who helped to fund the WDP over the years and who was a co-sponsor of the Hawaii-Diet™ Program.

- Ke Ola Mamo, the Native Hawaiian Health organization that has helped with the Hawaii Health Programs.

- Kenneth Brown; Robert Oshiro, Esq.; and the Queen Emma Foundation, who have always supported my efforts to promote health in Hawaii and around the world.

- Dr. Diane Nomura, the Administrator of the Hawaii Health Foundation, who has always helped to keep me and the foundation moving in the right direction.

- All the participants* in the HawaiiDiet™ Study who by their commitment helped to provide some of the scientific basis of the HawaiiDiet™.

- The Honorable Benjamin J. Cayetano, Governor of the State of Hawaii; Lt. Governor Mazie Hirono: members of the Governor's cabinet including Charles Toguchi, Susan Chandler, Herman Aizawa and Joseph Blanco; and State Senator Calvin Kawamoto who have committed themselves to help make this a success.

- All the participants* in the Hawaii Health Programs who by their participation helped to demonstrate the application of the science behind the program and bring it to the public.

- All the contributors* to the Hawaii Health Foundation, who by their generosity help us promote health and peace in Hawaii and eventually around the world. Special Thanks go to our major contributors: Hawaii Medical Service Association (HMSA), McInerny Foundation, Maybelle Roth, Frear Eleemosynary Trust, AlohaCare, and Bank of America.

- All the organizations and individuals* that supported us or our programs "in kind" such as: Waianae Coast Comprehensive Health Center; Ke Ola Mamo; Diagnostic Laboratory Services; Mokichi Okada Association; Ronald Sakamoto, Esq.; Hawaii State Department of Business; and Economic Development and Tourism.

- All the volunteers* of the Hawaii Health Foundation, who by their personal commitment and work have made many of the accomplishments of the Foundation possible.

- Jack Ha'o, my publisher; Jan Miller, my writer; and Jan Foster, my desktop publisher, who have helped me produce educational materials.

- Family and consumer science teachers Carol Devenot, Lynne Lee, and Jenny Choy, who have worked with me on recipes for these books.

- Barbara Burke, David McDonald, Janice Miller, Lindsey Pollock, and Ann Tang who helped edit the book.

- Lindsey Pollock, Lauree Nakata, and Carol Devenot who helped design the cover, and special thanks to Carol for the cover art and the chapter graphics.

I would also like to thank the following individuals and organizations who are at the top of their fields and were kind enough to take notice of our work; Robert Arnot, M.D. and NBC; Carolyn O'Neil and CNN; Laura Shapiro and *Newsweek*; Ben DiPietro, Meki Cox, and Associated Press; Dick Algire, Paula Akana, and KITV; Leslie Wilcox, Mary Zanakis, John Yoshimura, and KHON; Jade Moon and KGMB; Emmie Tomimbang; the TV show, "Lifestyle Magazine," Linda Tomchuck and *Encyclopedia Brittanica*; Barbara Ann Curcio and *Eating Well* magazine; *Vegetarian Times* magazine; Steven Pratt and the *Chicago Tribune*; *Tufts Newsletter*; Diana Sugg and the *Sacramento Bee*; Barbara Burke, Catherine Enomoto, Linda Hosek, Becky Ashizawa and the *Honolulu Star Bulletin*; Beverly Creamer, Chris Oliver, and the *Honolulu Advertiser*; Debbie Ward and *Ka Wai Ola o OHA*; Janice Otaguro and *Honolulu Magazine*; Ciel Sinnex and *MidWeek Magazine*; Sally-Jo Bowman and *Aloha Magazine*; Gwen Bataad and the *Hawaii Herald*; and many others whom I have forgotten to thank.

I would like to thank my *hanai* (adoptive) family, especially mom, Agnes Cope, and brother, Kamaki Kanahele, who have always given me wise counsel.

Thanks also to my brother, Arthur Shintani, and his company, Trends of Hawaii, who are always helping me with their support.

Thanks to my wife, Stephanie; daughters, Tracie and Nickie; and their grandparents, Henry and Peggy Hong, for their support and patience while I was writing this book.

Thanks to my parents, Emi and Robert Shintani, who are always with me in spirit.

Last but most important, I thank the Lord from whom all blessings and healings come forth.

---

* Names not listed because permission not obtained from all individuals.

৪১

Foreword .

All Things Are Connected

"In the beginning, God created the Heavens and the Earth."

In the Hawaiian chant of creation, "*The Kumulipo*," Sky Father *(Wakea)* and Earth Mother *(Papa)* mate and, through this mating create all things.

Similar creation beliefs are found in traditional cultures throughout the world, from the Asians to the Native Americans, from the ancient world through present times. The understanding that everything is born of a common source and therefore connected is fundamental to most of the great religions, philosophies, and traditional cultures of the world.

Modern day science is beginning to show us that when it came to issues of diet, lifestyle and spiritual faith, our ancestors were correct after all. The HawaiiDiet™ is a measured attempt to achieve good health by restoring these traditional values, diet, and lifestyle in a way which allows us to also make the most of modern science.

The HawaiiDiet™ was conceived in part as a response to the high rates of death from chronic diet-and-lifestyle-related diseases among the Native Hawaiians. Part of it began with my initial interest in traditional diet, and with my private practice. A major part of it began as the Waianae Diet Program in Waianae, Hawaii, a region that contains the largest native Hawaiian population in the world.

In the Waianae Coast community, there is great poverty from a material perspective. But the people there are also blessed with a great wealth from a spiritual perspective. The material poverty sets the stage for poor health. If nurtured properly, spiritual strength may set the stage for the recovery of good health. The success of the Waianae Diet Program is an example of the realization of some of this potential. Because of the dramatic improvement of the participants' health, and because of the ease with which most of them achieved weight loss, I have now received requests for the diet program from all over the world.

To be consistent with the Hawaiian spirit of *aloha* (which embraces all people), from the beginning, the program was intended to include people from all cultural backgrounds and to utilize foods and traditional cuisine from all cultural backgrounds. I have been using the same principles in private practice with people of all ethnic groups, with the same excellent results. This is a program that could be used and enjoyed by anybody, anywhere in the world.

It is called the "HawaiiDiet™ " in honor of the region where it was born, and also because of the spirit of the Hawaiian people. Their ancient wisdom embraces universal concepts common to traditional cultures from all over the world and, therefore, can provide a road map to world health and world peace.

Self-Experimentation and Traditional Diet

My first encounter with traditional diet was in the mid-1970s. I changed my diet at that time, in an attempt to improve my energy level. The results were astounding. My energy level increased dramatically and in a matter of days I went from sleeping 9 hours per day down to 5 hours per day. I lost 35 pounds effortlessly. I felt better than I had felt for years. I was following a strict vegetarian diet based on whole foods from traditional cultures around the world. *(Although my personal preference is still for a fully vegan diet, the HawaiiDiet™, while supporting the vegan diet, is not necessarily strictly vegetarian, in keeping with traditional practices of the common people around the world.)*

I was so surprised at what was happening to me that I began to seriously wonder: Why weren't the physicians and health care professionals at the university and in my community talking about the importance of diet in health and overall lifestyle success? Was there any hard scientific data that backed up what I sensed was happening to me?

These questions intrigued me to the point that I finally changed careers. I left the field of law and went to medical school. But medical school didn't offer much information with regard to nutrition or the *prevention* of disease. So after finishing medical school, I earned a master's degree in nutrition and, at the same time, became board certified in preventive medicine. Equipped with this new knowledge and information, I felt that I could truly be the best physician that I could possibly be.

Traditional Diet and Human Health

A major interest of mine had always been the effect of traditional diet and health around the world. I learned almost everywhere I looked that those cultures which were moving away from traditional diets were the same cultures that were rapidly developing epidemics of diet-related disease. Fortunately, studies began to emerge which indicated that many of these diet-related diseases could be reversed by returning people to their traditional, culture-based diet.

Furthermore, there was mounting evidence in the nutritional and preventive medicine communities that most common diseases in America could be both prevented and cured through a return to the traditional diet of our own ancestors, if done properly. The diseases which responded to diet-related therapies were such killers as heart disease, high cholesterol, high blood pressure, diabetes, hormone diseases, autoimmune diseases, gastrointestinal diseases, and many other chronic diseases which were reaching epidemic proportions in our society.

Putting Theory Into Practice

When I returned to Hawaii in 1987, I immediately began to apply the theory in private practice. My approach was to use diets that had no cholesterol and were about 10 percent fat, in keeping with my overall approach of modeling the program after typical ancient traditional diets. My goal was to use good diet and healthier lifestyles as a means of weaning people off of their medications and helping them avoid unnecessary surgeries. In general, I wanted to maximize the health and well-being of my patients, even those who did not show symptoms of an already established disease.

Shortly thereafter I also took a position at the Waianae Coast Comprehensive Health Center. I felt there was a great need there and that my background in nutrition would be useful in a population suffering from high rates of nutrition-related disease.

This center is the largest provider of primary health care to native Hawaiians in the world. At the WCCHC, we provide health care to some 10,000 Native Hawaiians. This population has many serious health problems, most of which are related to the modern American diet and lifestyle. The rate of obesity in this population is a staggering 64 percent. The rates of death from heart disease, cancer, stroke, and diabetes are among the highest in the nation.

At WCCHC, I was able to use the same approach that I used in private practice. But now I was working with a more select community. The Native Hawaiian people had long since abandoned their traditional diet, for a variety of reasons, but it was still possible to reconstruct that diet — unlike some cultures, which have become widely dispersed. I was given an opportunity to help the

Native Hawaiian people and others return to their traditional diet, which was infinitely more healthy than the Westernized diet which had taken its place.

Because I was working primarily with Native Hawaiians, I emphasized the use of traditional Hawaiian foods. I also added a community link to the program. Numerous people from the WCCHC and from the community at large helped to develop the program. This added a social support dimension to the program, and the blend enhanced the overall impact.

Ancient Ways For Modern Ills?

When the program was first being developed, I had few supporters. Some said the diet seemed too drastic. But because of the background I had already gained about traditional diets, I was convinced that the traditional Hawaiian diet would work in this community.

I was also convinced that the ancient Hawaiian cultural principles represented universal truths and that they were a key to getting people to maintain the diet and truly adopt a healthy lifestyle. I was blessed to be working for a community-owned health center that held the same conviction. The WCCHC board voted to allow me to spend time to develop this project despite the fact that we had no funds to support it. Fortunately, the Waianae Coast community came out to support the program and the project began with sheer *aloha* from the community. In addition, a catalyst to the Waianae Diet appeared. I became aware of a research project which held similar views to the Waianae Diet and was focusing on the traditional Hawaiian diet and its effect on serum lipids. This was the "Molokai Diet Study." This was the first research project to measure the effect of isocaloric traditional Hawaiian diet on lipids. Although the results were unpublished, the project provided credibility for the concept which I maintained, and it encouraged me to continue the course. In addition, the people who worked with the Molokai Diet, especially Claire Hughes, M.S., R.D., generously helped us with the development of our project and its coordinator, Helen Kanawaliwali O'Connor, became our coordinator. The combination of this assistance with the solid support of the Waianae Coast Comprehensive Health Center and the Waianae Coast community helped make this program possible.

Startling Results

When we finally implemented the program, it was a strict three-week, whole person program which used traditional Hawaiian foods and was based upon universal concepts of health as embodied in Hawaiian cultural healing principles. The results were startling. The average weight loss was 17 pounds in three weeks while people ate more food than before; cholesterol levels fell 14.1 percent. Some individuals' diabetes came under control so quickly that they had to be carefully monitored in the beginning while they were completely weaned off their insulin and other medication.

The results are published in the American Journal of Clinical Nutrition,[1] and the program won the highest national award for health promotion in the community from the U.S. Secretary of Health. We have been fortunate enough to have the program featured in Newsweek Magazine, on CNN news, on CBS, NBC, and in the Encyclopedia Britannica 1995 Health & Medical Annual, among other publications.

Why The HawaiiDiet™?

In 1997, I and others conducted a similar program known as the "HawaiiDiet™ Program" that provides some of the impetus for this book. The participants of the program included the Governor of the State of Hawaii, the Honorable Benjamin J. Cayetano, and other community leaders including members of the Hawaiian Homestead known as Papakolea. The results of their program were even more remarkable with cholesterol falling an average of 24 percent in just a matter of 3 weeks.

The HawaiiDiet™ is a presentation of the concept I have been working with for these many years, but it is targeted at a general audience so that it may benefit as many people as possible. As I described, it is based on universal principles embodied in traditional Hawaiian concepts. This includes concepts such as *lokahi*, or "wholeness"; and a*loha*, or the "universal love," which embraces people of all cultures. Thus, the HawaiiDiet™ may be practiced by anyone, anywhere in the world.

Transition to a Vegetarian Diet

Many of my readers know that I am vegetarian despite the fact that some of the diets I work with are not necessarily vegetarian. The basis of the HawaiiDiet™ is in part traditional cultural eating patterns from around the world and most of these diets included flesh albeit a very small amount *(roughly 1 ounce per day)*. In fact, this low a consumption of flesh suggests that the vast majority of modern humans were primarily vegetarian most of the time. The HawaiiDiet™ reflects this eating pattern for the first two weeks and in the last week is a strictly vegetarian *(plant-based)* diet. This provides a convenient transition to a plant-based diet. The readers should know unambiguously that the HawaiiDiet™ encourages a whole-food plant-based diet as ideal for optimal health, except under unusual circumstances.

As for the use of other nonessential food items such as oil and sweeteners, the HawaiiDiet™ takes some liberties in their use in keeping with traditional dietary food patterns. There should be no mistake that the HawaiiDiet™ does not consider these foods to be ideal and recommends minimal use of these items. We at the Hawaii Health Foundation feel that the focus on traditional diets as a model for this book will attract the interest of a much broader segment of the population and ultimately reduce the consumption of animal products to a greater extent than if we were to remain with a strict vegan agenda. Our preliminary results indicate that this approach still yields excellent health outcomes (see Chapter 2), and early reports of individuals such as the Governor's son adopting a vegetarian lifestyle as a result of the HawaiiDiet™ indicates that this strategy for promoting a plant-based diet in general is effective as well.

An Invitation

I invite you to try the HawaiiDiet™ and see if you might improve your health and lose some excess pounds. Perhaps you might become part of a movement to restore not only your own health, but also the health of the community and ultimately the health of the whole world.

ဆ

Chapter 1
Introduction

"The results are miraculous: some
of Dr. Shintani's patients sound as
though they've been to Lourdes."
[Laura Shapiro, Newsweek, August 9, 1993]

Take the First Step Toward
Changing Your Life

Congratulations. By picking up this book, you have
taken the first step toward changing your life. You have
picked up this book for a reason, and I don't believe in
accidents. So please read on.

The purpose of this cookbook is to help you maximize your health and minimize your weight. It will give
you a new perspective on health by letting you look
through the lens of some universal principles embodied
in a few basic Hawaiian concepts. It will also provide
you with a step-by-step nutrition plan, complete with
many delicious recipes. This program is designed so you
can make it part of your life.

Many Others Have Succeeded: So Can You!

In these pages, you'll see that others are succeeding at this program, or have already succeeded. People such as Mary T., whose heart-warming story is representative of what this diet can do for you.

Mary is one of the "miracles" that Ms. Laura Shapiro mentioned in the Newsweek article about the program.

At age 40, Mary was already taking 80 units of insulin and she was at high risk for serious complications from the disease. She went on the HawaiiDiet™. She soon lost 51 pounds. Seven years later, she maintains that same weight although she "eats everything in sight."

Five days after Mary started Dr. Shintani's program, she stopped her twice-a-day insulin injections (under very close physicians' supervision) and hasn't needed one since. She says, "I have more energy, I sleep less. This diet has literally changed my life."

Hawaii's Leaders Take the Lead

On the HawaiiDiet™, Hawaii's Governor Benjamin Cayetano reduced his cholesterol from 234 mg/dl down to 162 mg/dl. His "good cholesterol" increased from 26 to 32. His triglyceride fell 516 points from 617 mg/dl to a normal level of 83 mg/dl *(normal is 50 to 150 mg/dl)*.

Ellen K.

And then there is Ellen K., who told me: "This is the greatest diet in the world," as she stepped on my office scale. She had lost 60 pounds after years of failing on every other diet. She looked better than she had in years, her skin was glowing, and she had new vitality and a renewed zest for life.

There are many others, far too many to list here. These few testimonials are just a representation of what is possible with the HawaiiDiet™.

What's In This Diet For You?

What, exactly, can you expect from this health program? In this simple step-by-step plan, this book will help you:

- Lose weight without counting calories or portion sizes;

- Learn how to select foods that help you lose weight;

- Maximize your health;

- Minimize your need for medications;

- Increase your energy level;

- Provide you with a new perspective on health that will help you stay healthy for a lifetime;

- Provide you with delicious recipes that will make the meals a pleasure.

If you are like most people, you've probably already tried dieting, only to find that it doesn't work in the long run. For most people, even if they do lose weight it returns as soon as they step away from the iron-clad discipline that most diet regimens require.

This program is not a diet in the conventional sense of the word. It is, rather, a health program that shows you how to lose weight by maximizing your health without so-called dieting. Whereas most weight loss diets rely upon deprivation and rigorous willpower, the Hawaii-Diet™ Program utilizes your natural enjoyment of eating. It shows you how to replace unhealthy, fat-promoting foods with healthy, delicious foods which satisfy in every way.

Or perhaps you are more concerned about your health than about your weight. Maybe you are battling a health problem such as high blood pressure, high cholesterol, or maybe a touch of diabetes. Or you may just not feel up to par and you want your health back. In any case, the HawaiiDiet™ makes it possible for you to eat all the delicious food you want, of any ethnic cuisine, while still losing weight and restoring your health.

What Is the HawaiiDiet™?

1.   The HawaiiDiet™ Is a Whole Person Program.

The HawaiiDiet™ includes the enhancement of the health of the whole person, including spiritual, mental, emotional and physical aspects, through the focus on food and diet. It includes exercise, stress reduction, and a perspective on life and health based on an understanding of universal principles as embodied in traditional Hawaiian concepts and a faith in God. When all of these aspects are in harmony, your health is maximized. And when your health is maximized, your excess weight disappears automatically. Energy levels increase and you become more effective in every way. You may even notice a measure of spiritual growth that may affect you in very personal ways.

2.   The HawaiiDiet™ Is a No-deprivation Eating Program.

There is no calorie counting or portion size restriction on the HawaiiDiet™. It is an "all you can eat" health program that emphasizes the type of food eaten rather than the quantity of food eaten. In fact, in our studies, people wind up eating MORE food than ever and still lose weight. For more information about the science behind this phenomenon, please refer to my books: *Dr.*

Shintani's Eat More, Weigh Less® Diet and *Dr. Shintani's Eat More, Weigh Less® Cookbook.*

3. The HawaiiDiet™ Integrates Modern Science with Ancient Wisdom.

The HawaiiDiet™ employs the best of both worlds: it seeks to integrate ancient wisdom with modern science. Leading edge research from nutritionists and physicians is beginning to support the value of the HawaiiDiet's™ approach. New information on the benefits of eating whole grains, vegetables and fruit is a lesson in why our ancestors rarely suffered from chronic, diet-related diseases that plague us today, nor did they have problems with obesity. They knew something that we are only beginning to relearn. Therefore, while the HawaiiDiet™ is grounded in good science, it looks to ancient wisdom found in traditional Hawaiian principles and employs this wisdom as a compass for the present HawaiiDiet™ Program, as well as for future research.

4. The HawaiiDiet™ Is Based Upon Traditional Eating Patterns.

In my research into traditional diets, I began to see patterns established with regard to the traditional/ ancient diets of the healthiest, longest-living cultures. With few exceptions, the healthiest traditional cultures ate a diet similar to that of the ancient Hawaiians in macro-nutrient content, and also practiced lifestyle principles similar to those of ancient Hawaii. This made it easy to draw upon the wisdom of the ancient Hawaiians to provide an example of optimum diet and lifestyle practices. Therefore, Hawaii is used as a model for many traditional cultures: the diet and lifestyle principles are basic to those of most other ethnic groups, with few variations in regional tastes, food availability, and cultural practices. To simplify the application of this concept, a diagram known as the "HawaiiDiet™ Pyramid" is used to assist in the selection of types and combinations of foods. The diet is high in whole complex carbohydrates, very low in fat, has little or no cholesterol, and is high in plant-based foods.

In the three-week "Hawaii Health Program," the first two weeks contained an average of one ounce of flesh per day. This reflects the fact that traditional cultural diets, such as ancient Asian diets, included roughly this amount of flesh. In the third week, the diet was strictly vegetarian. This reflects the fact that most humans ate no flesh on most days. At least from the perspective of heart disease, a plant-based diet is ideal.

5. The HawaiiDiet™ Is Not "One-Diet-Fits-All" Program.

Because the HawaiiDiet™ is based on traditional diets from many cultures, it recognizes that some individuals may be adapted to different dietary patterns than others. For example, a higher fat Mediterranean-style diet may be acceptable in individuals who are adapted to such a diet. The HawaiiDiet™ allows for the tailoring of the diet to fit individual needs and genetic make up.

However, for the purpose of weight control, the very low-fat "Hawaii Pacific" pattern seems to be the most effective. Moreover, for the purpose of cholesterol control, a no cholesterol diet appears to be the most effective. Thus, a very low fat, no cholesterol dietary pattern is encouraged and the HawaiiDiet™ provides an excellent transition in that direction.

6. The HawaiiDiet™ Uses Foods That Are Commonly Available.

Because the HawaiiDiet™ embraces traditional eating patterns from cultures around the world, the choices of foods are virtually endless. The diet can be made of foods that are available in your local supermarket and are simple to prepare, or it can be made of foods that are exotic and prepared by a gourmet chef. Thus, the HawaiiDiet™ can be used by anyone and incorporated into their lifestyle for the rest of their lives.

7. The HawaiiDiet™ Is High in Mass Index.

The "Mass Index of Food," or "SMI," (which stands for the Shintani Mass Index of Food) is a new concept in the evaluation of the weight-loss-inducing effect of food.

It is also known as the "Eat More Index," or "EMI," described in my other book, the original *Dr. Shintani's Eat More, Weigh Less® Diet.* I'll just give you a thumbnail sketch here (see pages 42 to 45 for a fuller description). The SMI is one of the tools which will simplify the diet for you and which will make it easy to stick with the HawaiiDiet™ for the rest of your life. This index is a food table found at the back of this book and in greater detail in *Dr. Shintani's Eat More, Weigh Less® Diet* book, which distills the quality and quantity of any given food down to one easy-to-read number.

Low-SMI foods are generally low in mass-to-energy ratio and will lend themselves to weight gain because you have to consume a lot of calories in order to get enough food mass to feel full. In addition, most low-SMI foods are generally unhealthy, because they tend to be higher in fat, sugar, and other unhealthy food ingredients. However, high-SMI foods have a high mass-to-energy ratio. You can eat a reasonable amount of them and feel totally satisfied and nourished, because they generally contain better nutrition in addition to a better energy-to-calorie ratio.

These seven elements of the HawaiiDiet™ form the basics. Now let's take a look at how this all works for you.

No More Deprivation,
No Counting Calories

During the course of this program, you will focus upon the positive aspects of health and weight control. This means you will not be worried about deprivation, and you won't be focusing upon all the things you should not do. No more counting calories, no more concern about the portion sizes of your food. Instead, you *will* be focused upon all the delicious meals and recipes which have been carefully selected for you. You will be focused on foods that satisfy your hunger: foods which you can obtain in your local supermarket, simple foods which you can continue eating and enjoying for the rest of your life.

It is important that you remember that there is no restriction upon who can succeed at this program. Even though the HawaiiDiet™ was conceived partially in response to the high rates of death from chronic diet-and-lifestyle-related disease among the Native Hawaiians, the same health crisis is occurring right now in America as a whole. Nearly 70 percent of us are dying from diet-and-lifestyle-related diseases. And, thus, the same basic diet-and-lifestyle principles apply to us all.

With the HawaiiDiet™ Program, you can discover how to optimize your health no matter what your age, sex, ethnic makeup, or regional background.

How Easy Is the HawaiiDiet™?

How easy is it to make a quick meal at home? How easy is it to dine on the inventions of some of the best chefs in Paradise? In the recipe section, you'll find a whole range of dishes, from simple to gourmet. In addition to home-cooking recipes and fast food recipes, you'll also find dishes from Roy Yamaguchi, Peter Merriman, and Mark Ellman — all world-class chefs. You'll also find recipes from some of Hawaii's family and consumer science teachers, who also offer up a cornucopia of home-spun dishes and first-class cuisine. And you'll find delicious, traditional foods from all cultures — a reflection of the wonderful diversity of Hawaii's multicultural society.

Most of the recipes are selected for their ease of preparation and for the availability of the ingredients. Whether you're a seasoned cook or just a beginner, you'll find something here that works for you.

You can make your recipe choices based on the HawaiiDiet™ Pyramid, and based upon the "SMI." With the range of recipes and these two handy program aids, you'll soon find yourself eating mouth-watering meals based on many cultures' cuisines from Hawaiian-Pacific, to European, to Asian, to the rest of the world.

℘

Chapter 2
The Results of the HawaiiDiet™

In order to demonstrate the effectiveness of the HawaiiDiet™, we put a number of community leaders, including the Governor and some representatives of the Native Hawaiian community of Papakolea Homestead, on the HawaiiDiet™ in a 3-week program.

In 3 weeks, the group weight loss for the 23 participants was 249.25 pounds. Average weight loss per person was 10.8 pounds. The highest weight loss was 21.75 pounds.

Average cholesterol decreased 23.6% *(from an average of 205 mg/dl to 157 mg/dl)*. At the beginning of the program, there were 11 people with cholesterol over 200. At the end of the program there was only one person whose cholesterol was over 200.

Average triglycerides decreased 36.3% from an average of 238 mg/dl to 152 mg/dl *(normal range – 50 mg/dl to 150 mg/dl)*. One person's triglycerides decreased 863 mg/dl from 988 mg/dl to 125 mg/dl. Another person's triglycerides decreased from 617 mg/dl to 93 mg/dl.

Blood sugar in those with diabetes or borderline diabetes fell an average of 38%, from an average of 177 mg/dl to 122 mg/dl. This drop resulted even though the four participants on medication for diabetes were able to reduce their medications, including one who got off 90 units of insulin.

Average blood pressure fell from 130/79 to 120/75. This resulted even after eliminating one person's blood pressure medication when his blood pressure dropped to normal levels, and also after reducing the blood pressure medication of two other people.

The following diagram indicates the average results of the 23 participants.

The Hawaii Health Program

Results After 21 Days on the "Hawaii Diet"

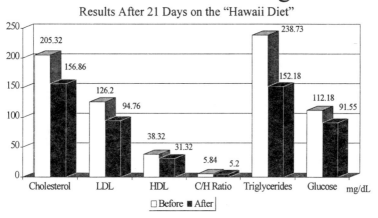

Chapter 3
Ancient Ways for Modern Health

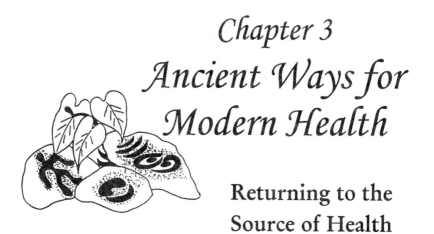

Returning to the Source of Health

In addition to being consistent with modern science, the HawaiiDiet™ is guided by universal values as embodied in traditional Hawaiian principles.

If we could regain the simple understanding of spirit and nature which was common to our ancestors, we would once again be able to solve the devastating epidemic of chronic diseases which kill most of us. These diseases were not even an issue during ancient times. In the modern, developed world, these major killer diseases are linked to diet and lifestyle. We can learn much by simply realizing that most of these diseases were seldom if ever a problem for our ancestors, simply because their diet and lifestyles were in harmony with their environment.

Unfortunately, our diets and lifestyles have significantly changed since ancient times. Our high-tech society offers solutions to certain problems, such as medical intervention in trauma situations, antibiotics and vaccines, and other similar achievements. At the same time it creates other, less obvious problems which contribute to such devastation as heart disease, cancer, diabetes, and other diet and lifestyle-related disease.

These are, not incidentally, the very health problems which the HawaiiDiet™ best addresses. And we must all address these fundamental problems, if we are ever to heal our people.

Toward this end, we must regain a basic understanding of nature and the underlying cause of disease. This healing must begin with individuals, then broaden to include our communities, our nation and ultimately the problems of this Earth itself.

The Solution

The underlying solution to all these problems can be found in a return to traditional ways. We can and should regain the basic understanding of our ancestors, whether they be from Hawaii, Europe, Asia, Africa, the Americas, or the myriad islands all over the world. These universal principles are embodied in the Hawaiian culture and, in these pages, you will learn the Hawaiian version of what are often universal, ancient, traditional cultural belief systems. You will recognize the underlying humanity and value in the ancient Hawaiian wisdom and, if you wish, you can adapt this to your own modern life.

If we are ever to solve the many problems we listed above, we must not only return to traditional values. We must also return to the diet(s) which our bodies were designed to use as the optimal fuel if we are to escape the physical and emotional imbalances or impaired thinking processes that undermine our ability to adhere to the values which we esteem and aspire toward.

Principles of the HawaiiDiet™

1. Hawaii

Hawaii has become a place where people come for healing. The word *"Hawai'i"* translated to English means, "the breath *(ha)* and water *(wai)* of life from God *(i)*" — a perfect formula for health.

2. *Lokahi:* "Oneness, unity."

The central principle to understand is *lokahi*. *Lokahi* literally means "consensus." From a health perspective it means "harmony," "oneness," "wholeness" and that "all things are connected." In the deepest sense, *lokahi* means that "we are connected to everyone and everything — whether person, land, or the larger universe."

If we understand this principle, we begin to understand the wisdom of the ages. This principle is a fundamental piece of the fabric of all the great cultures of the world and is the foundation of Hawaiian healing. In modern times, we have forgotten this principle. If we internalize this principle and begin to incorporate it in our thoughts, actions, and prayers, we will make some startling and revealing conclusions about health and how we may heal ourselves.

For example, if we understand *lokahi*, we will realize that because of this interconnectedness, our total health ultimately depends upon the health of our spiritual, mental, emotional and physical being. It is also dependent on the health of our relationship to the environment and everyone around us. And, with regard to diet, health is intimately related to what we eat. Through the principle of *lokahi*, we are connected to that food. In the most literal, physical sense, we become what we eat.

If we understand *lokahi*, we will also realize that the optimal solution to health involves healing the whole person and not just giving a certain pill or cutting out a part of the body. We must first seek to find the reason for the illness. In fact, we must know the meaning of early symptoms. Simply taking pills and forgetting about the disease is NOT the answer. Such a simplistic response almost always neglects the true cause of the disease and neglects the whole-person aspects of health. The result is that the solution remains incomplete, and typically, the underlying disease remains, with its symptoms covered up. Instead, if we simply apply the concept of *lokahi* or "wholeness," we would see that most of today's modern illnesses are caused by our own actions, not only as individuals but also as a society. Knowing this, we should begin to shape our attitudes and plans towards changing the way we maintain health and how we deliver health care.

Lokahi and Diet

The concept of *lokahi* when applied to diet gives us one of the most fundamental principles of the Hawaii-Diet™. It points out that if we are to be as healthy or as "whole" as possible, then the food we eat should be as "whole" as possible as well. In other words, whole grains are preferred over whole grain flour, and whole grain flour is preferred over white refined flour or sugar. In the HawaiiDiet™, the food table described as a "Food Mass Index" *(SMI or EMI)* helps us select foods that would be more whole. By using this table, people find that their weight comes off naturally.

Once we know the relationship between the concept of *lokahi* and health, we are on our way to health. The next step is to know what to do about it. This process is begun when we begin to understand the meaning of *pono*.

3. *Pono*

Pono means "justice or righteousness." From the perspective of health, it means that if we establish *pono* or "righteousness" in relation to the laws of the universe that govern our health, disease will disappear and health will be restored. This includes eating the right foods, thinking the right thoughts, and doing the right things, always with *aloha* in our hearts and always mindful of the gifts of life and health that God has given us. When we are not "righteous" in our ways, consequences result due to the forces of nature and "justice" is restored.

For example, in America, we center our diet on animal products. What is considered our "main dish" is beef, pork, chicken, fish, or other flesh foods. Throughout the history of humanity, the great civilizations never ate this way. The traditional ways of eating were always centered on a starchy staple product that served as the principal food and an abundance of vegetables. Thus, our current way of eating is not *pono*, not in "harmony" with nature or tradition. In fact, we as a nation in our greedy fashion kill and eat so many animals that we are in great disharmony — far out of balance with nature. The forces of nature exact natural justice and restore *pono* by returning to humans a terrible toll: Death. As humans are the leading cause of death of animals *(because we slaughter them for food)*, animals are the leading cause of death of humans *(because we eat them, and we pay a massive price in heart attacks, strokes and cancers)*.

In the same way, by the principle of *pono*, what we do positively comes back to us in a positive way. Once we apply this principle of *pono* and re-establish it in our whole selves, including spiritual, mental, emotional, and physical aspects, we improve our health. If we do it properly, ailments naturally disappear and we begin to feel much better than before. If we eat and live in harmony with our environment according to the traditional cultural ways of our ancestors, health returns. This is why the HawaiiDiet™ is based on traditional cultural ways of eating. The HawaiiDiet™ Pyramid provides a guide to doing this. Our research demonstrates a dramatic improvement of health in those who follow this way of eating.

In another context, by the principle of *pono*, giving and receiving are the same. This is why the concept of *aloha*, which is the "giving of unconditional love," is a major key in one's own health and happiness; because eventually all the love that you give comes back to you.

4. *Aloha*

The common meaning of *aloha* is the well known salutation of "hello," "goodbye," or "love." In a deeper sense it means "universal love" — the love for everyone and the embracing of all people, creatures, and things. It is the spirit of loving unconditionally and giving unconditionally that characterizes the Hawaiian spirit. The deeper spiritual translation of *aloha* is "the joining of heaven and earth" *(alo)* and "breath of life" *(ha)*. Together it is a powerful statement of wishing that the forces of nature and the spirit of God be with someone.

Although *aloha* has many usages, all usages stem from the concept of universal love. Universal love permeates the fundamental spirit of Hawaiian culture. It is an inherently nonjudgmental culture, and therefore the ways of all cultures are embraced, respected, and accepted. What is therefore known as the "*aloha* spirit," a title which has been made mundane by overusage, is in fact largely responsible for the multicultural harmony now found in Hawaii. Many cultures have migrated to Hawaii from all over the world. Though most outsiders see Hawaii as a tropical paradise, with somewhat unsophisticated people, Hawaii is among the most cosmopolitan of all places in the world, with a preponderance of well-educated, well-traveled people. Hawaii is often described as a cultural "melting pot." I prefer to call it a cultural "tossed salad," where the blend works well and creates a delightful mix of flavors, yet each individual cultural flavor remains unique. You will see this principle reflected in the multicultural nature of the recipes in this cookbook, and in the HawaiiDiet™ Program.

If we make these principles a part of our lives and optimize our health based on the application of these principles, we may undergo an inner transformation. We begin to intuitively understand nature and the universe much as our ancestors did. As a result, we have some insight into the true nature of things. Our bodies, minds and spirits begin to resonate with nature. We then begin to realize that there is a "spirit" or a "life force" in everything and every living creature — that in everything, in everyone, there is *mana*.

5. *Mana*

Mana means life force or spiritual energy in people and things. Once again this is a universal concept found in the great civilizations of the world. In China, it was called *"chi."* In Japan, it was called *"ki."* In India, it was called *"prana,"* and in the Christian religion it was simply the "spirit of God in all people and things."

This life force was recognized in all things, whether animate or inanimate: a force akin to the more Westernized belief that there is a spiritual world that lies beyond all things physical and which plays itself out on the physical stage. The spiritual, unseen aspects of everyone and everything were respected. For example: in Hawaiian tradition, if you offered food to a passing stranger, you were in fact offering food to the spirit of God within that person. This is a beautiful concept, comparable to the biblical passage: "Let brotherly love continue. Do not forget to entertain strangers, for by so doing some have unwittingly entertained angels." (*Hebrews 13:1,2, NKJV*)

If we regain the understanding that the ancient Hawaiians possessed of the nature of the universe, we would see the answer to many difficult problems that afflict our society today. The failing health of America and other modernizing nations is one of the problems. In ancient Hawaii, the idea of a "life force" in all beings and things was second nature. If we begin to come to this realization, then many of the principles of the Hawaii-Diet™ also become intuitive and an integral part of our being.

Once we fully understand these five concepts:

> *Hawai'i,* "the breath and water of life
> *lokahi,* "oneness"
> *pono,* "righteousness"
> *aloha,* "universal love"
> *mana,* "life force,"

we can begin to learn what to do with them. First, we can incorporate this way of understanding into our lives. The realization of the existence of *mana* in food helps keep us motivated to stay on the HawaiiDiet™. We learn the ancient Hawaiian arts of manifesting reality on earth so that we can all enhance our contribution to all of life within God's plan. This technique or concept is called *'ano 'ano*.

6. *'Ano 'Ano*

'Ano 'ano literally means "seed." In the Hawaii-Diet™, there are several underlying meanings to this word. When used to refer to the ancient creation myths, it means "the seed of all things."

The "seed" concept is also biblical. The parable of the mustard seed is one example. The biblical tenets to plant seeds of faith, of love, are found throughout the Holy Book. In what is known as "The Parable of the Seed" in Luke, Chapter 8, we are in fact told that the very Word of God is "seed." And the human body is also described as the seed which will ultimately become pure spirit, in I Corinthians, Chapter 15.

In most Hawaiian teaching, this concept describes a method used by some *kahunas*, or priests, to help create a reality by planting a seed of thought in one's mind and nurturing it into physical reality. It is similar to what we could now call visualization.

This was a seven-step process. In the first step, one had to be sure that an action was in harmony with God's plan. If we are to achieve anything of true value in this world, we must first be sure that the plan is *pono* or "righteous" in the Lord's eyes. The seven steps are as follows:

1. Sit quietly and search your soul, see truly what it is you desire, then make sure it is in harmony with God's plan. Pray, and if it is in God's plan, He will give you what you ask.

2. Ask for guidance to ensure that what you want is good for all involved.

3. State clearly in detail the condition that you want with words, numbers, data. Be specific about what you want.

4. See this end result in full detail with color, sound and action. Remember, ". . . faith is the substance of things hoped for, the evidence of things not seen." *[Hebrews 11:1]*

5. Feel what it will be like to have this desired result come to fruition.

6. Do not tell others about the seed you have planted until fruition. It is enough that God knows.

7. Pray for the results each day with the words you have chosen and give gratitude as you see and feel this result as already accomplished.

These seven steps are powerful. Knowing how to make them work is a great responsibility and it must only be used with the understanding of the principles described above: *lokahi*, "we are all connected"; *pono*, "we must exercise these powers with righteousness"; *aloha*, "we must do this work with universal love"; and *mana*, "there is an unseen life force, i.e., the spirit of God in everything."

Most of all, we must exercise these seven steps to further worthy objectives that fall within God's plan, for in the end all else is meaningless.

Finally, if we do these things with faith "the size of a mustard seed," all things shall be possible. And then, in coming full circle, *we* become the "seed" — the *'ano 'ano* for the future of health and peace in our communities and the world.

ၶ

Chapter 4
Making the
HawaiiDiet™ Work For You

Practical Principles of the HawaiiDiet™

The HawaiiDiet™ can work for you on many levels. Remember, if you have any health problems or are on any medications, check with your doctor before changing your diet. He or she will want to monitor how any changes may affect you if you are on medication or are otherwise in very poor health.

After you've done that, or if you don't need to, take a moment to carefully contemplate the following suggestions. Even though these aren't all strictly dietary principles, if you integrate them into your program it will work better, and you'll enjoy it more. You'll also be far more likely to make the HawaiiDiet™ a permanent part of your lifestyle, so you can enjoy the results of weight loss and improved health all the rest of your days.

1. First, if you have any health problems, check with your doctor to make sure that it's okay to follow this diet. If you are taking any medication, it is

especially important that you check with your doctor to see if you need to be monitored for medication adjustments.

2. Next, understand the basic principles of the Hawaii-Diet™ including the cultural principles such as *lokahi* as described in this book. Understand that everything is connected and that our food affects our health, our work performance, our emotions, and even our spiritual development.

3. Eat the way our ancestors ate. Enjoy the multicultural cuisine of the HawaiiDiet™, using the Hawaii-Diet™ Pyramid as your guide.

4. Eat foods in their whole form as much as possible. Use the Shintani Mass Index of Food *(also known as SMI)* as a way to assist in the selection of these foods.

5. Keep your cholesterol intake to zero or very low. The HawaiiDiet™ encourages a plant-based diet and if you must use flesh foods, it should be no more than an average of one ounce per day.

6. Keep the fat content very low *(around 10% of calories),* unless there is some evidence that you can handle a higher fat diet. Remember that the fat should come from whole plant-based sources, if possible.

7. Eat foods in harmony with the seasons, your locality, and your climate. If possible eat fresh, whole, plant-based foods grown organically.

8. Eat in a relaxed manner, preferably with others. Take time to chew and enjoy your food — do so with gratitude.

9. Exercise at least 30 to 40 minutes daily, or at least every other day.

10. Remember that optimal health involves all aspects of your being. This includes spiritual, mental, emotional, and physical aspects. It includes your thoughts and actions, and your relationship with the land through the food you eat. It includes your relationship with others and your relationship with the Almighty. When all this is in harmony, stress is reduced and health is maximized.

There are a number of simple things you can do to reduce stress and contribute to your overall health. For example:

- Say a prayer daily;

- Meditate daily;

- Laugh daily;

- Sing a happy song every day;

- Do something for someone else, with no expectation of reward.

11. Always remember where the healing comes from. It comes from the Almighty. Therefore, say a grace before each meal. Start each meal by asking the Lord to bless the food and be grateful for the life-giving qualities which he has put into the food that you eat.

12. In addition to saying grace, pray and meditate each day to enhance your connection to the Source.

What To Expect When You Begin the HawaiiDiet™

The HawaiiDiet™ is not a diet at all. There is no calorie counting or any portion size control on the diet. It is an "all you can eat" diet. This doesn't mean that you should stuff yourself unnaturally on this diet. However, it does mean that you can eat to your satisfaction and even more than you were eating before, and the weight comes off naturally.

You may experience a little sensation of bloating in the beginning because in general the foods are bulkier than what most Americans are accustomed to eating. This should add to a pleasant feeling of satisfaction throughout the diet, even while you are losing the pounds. It is actually a whole person health program, based on the principles and practices of traditional cultures that have remained largely free of the chronic, nutrition-related diseases that plague us today.

You will probably be exposed to a wider variety of foods on this diet than you have previously enjoyed. This is because the HawaiiDiet™ embraces foods from all cultures that fit the HawaiiDiet™ model. The potential variety is limitless.

How Much Will I Lose?

The weight loss is dramatic in some individuals. It is slow and steady in others. People have lost as much as 30 pounds in 21 days. Your personal weight loss will depend upon your beginning weight and your individual metabolism, as well as upon other individual factors. In general, your weight loss should range from 5 to 30 pounds in the first 3 weeks of the diet. Average weight loss has been around 11 pounds for this time. When followed strictly, no one who is overweight has failed to lose weight on this program.

Health Changes

For those who have health problems, changes may be dramatic. **Be sure to check with your doctor if you have any health problems**, as we have previously suggested. People on the HawaiiDiet™ have experienced dramatic improvement in their blood sugar, blood pressure, and in countless symptoms. Participants have indicated that such symptoms as headaches, joint pains, fatigue, skin conditions, gastrointestinal complaints, and numerous other symptoms have improved with their change to the HawaiiDiet™. In addition, serum levels of cholesterol, triglycerides, uric acids, and other health entities have improved.

What About Later?

The HawaiiDiet™ is designed to be a whole lifestyle program: one which will forever change the ways in which you understand your food and your relationship to it.

In our experience, developing an understanding of the principles that we describe in this book greatly enhances the likelihood of people keeping the weight off in the long run. The recipes will also serve you well. You will be able to make choices ranging from simple recipes to gourmet treats, with a delicious variety of culinary styles.

For additional support and information, you may want to read my *Dr. Shintani's Eat More, Weigh Less® Diet* book, which explains in greater depth why this program induces weight loss without calorie restriction. You may also wish to read and use my *Dr. Shintani's Eat More, Weigh Less® Cookbook*, which offers you 77 tips on how to make your HawaiiDiet™ fast and tasty, and which shows you how to keep it low in fat. It also offers you

177 delicious cholesterol-free recipes you can use on this diet.

The HawaiiDiet™ Pyramid

An important tool of the HawaiiDiet™ is the HawaiiDiet™ Pyramid. I created this pyramid by modifying the USDA "Food Guide Pyramid," to make it a little healthier.

The USDA's Food Guide Pyramid
A Guide to Daily Food Choices

The USDA "Food Guide Pyramid" is itself an improvement over the old "Four Food Groups" dietary recommendation. But, in my opinion and that of many scientists, it is not good enough. Here is what it looks like:

One key reason for the modification was the USDA's emphasis on dairy and meat, as you can see in the USDA pyramid, above. In my opinion *(and in the opinion of many other scientists)*, the USDA is much too liberal with dairy and meat groups from the perspective of preventing heart disease, certain cancers, and certain other chronic diseases. Compare it to:

The Hawaii Diet Pyramid
A Guide to Daily Food Choices

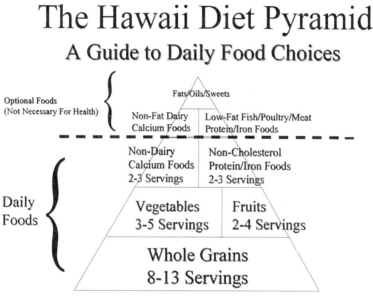

Optional Foods
(Not Necessary For Health)

Fats/Oils/Sweets

Non-Fat Dairy Calcium Foods | Low-Fat Fish/Poultry/Meat Protein/Iron Foods

Non-Dairy Calcium Foods 2-3 Servings | Non-Cholesterol Protein/Iron Foods 2-3 Servings

Daily Foods

Vegetables 3-5 Servings | Fruits 2-4 Servings

Whole Grains 8-13 Servings

(c) Shintani 1993

By contrast, the HawaiiDiet™ Pyramid, used in conjunction with the Shintani's Mass Index of Food (SMI), addresses both health and weight loss in a simple and practical way.

Understanding the HawaiiDiet™ Pyramid

The HawaiiDiet™ Pyramid is a diagram which provides a way to help ensure that the nutrients you obtain from food are adequate. The following table shows how the HawaiiDiet™ Pyramid differs from the USDA pyramid. I recommend the modified HawaiiDiet™ Pyramid as your guide for daily use.

Food Groups	USDA Food Guide Pyramid Guidelines *(servings)*	HawaiiDiet™ Pyramid Guidelines *(servings)*
Grains	6 - 11	8 - 13
Vegetables	3 - 5	3 - 5
Fruit	2 - 4	2 - 4
Non-Dairy Calcium Foods (replaces dairy)		2 - 3
Non-cholesterol Protein/ Iron Foods (replaces meat)		2 - 3
Dairy	2-3	never or rarely
Meat/Fish/Poultry	2-3	never or rarely
Fats/Oils/Sweets	sparingly	never or rarely

What Is a Serving?

A "serving" is an amount of selected food which an average person might serve at a single sitting. This is actually a somewhat arbitrary definition because how much a person may serve of certain foods varies a great deal. Nonetheless, the term provides a starting point. Here are examples of "servings":

Cereal and Grains Group

1/2 cup of cooked cereal, pasta, or brown rice;
1 slice of bread; or 1 ounce of ready-to-eat cereal

Vegetable Group

1 cup of raw leafy greens; 1/2 cup of cooked,
chopped, raw, or other vegetables

Fruit Group

1 medium fruit; 1/2 cup of chopped,
cooked, or canned fruit

Dairy Group

1 cup of milk, yogurt, or ice cream; 1-1/2 ounce
of cheese; or 2 ounces processed cheese

Beans, Fish, Poultry, Meat Group

1/2 cup of cooked beans; 2 to 3 ounces of
cooked fish, chicken, or meat; 1 egg

What's New?

Notice the changes in the pyramid. I have made the
fats/oils/sugar section smaller. Then I minimized the
dairy and meat foods and moved them into the tip of the
HawaiiDiet™ Pyramid as optional/occasional foods. In
place of the Dairy Group, I created a Non-Dairy Calcium Group. In place of the Meat Group, I created a
Non-cholesterol Protein/Iron Group.

Vegetarian Diet is Ideal

Notice also that the HawaiiDiet™ Pyramid is separated by a dotted line at the apex. The foods above the line are foods not necessary for good health for most people. It is preferable not to use them except in certain circumstances or health conditions. If you do use them, do so sparingly and with the knowledge that they are not ideal for optimal health. You should eat no more than an average of 1 ounce of flesh per day, if you want to follow traditional cultural eating patterns. This reflects the fact that animal foods were not eaten on a daily basis among Mediterranean and Asian people, who rarely suffer from the diseases that plague us today, such as heart disease. It is consistent with modern literature, which indicates that a vegetarian diet is typically healthier than a diet with daily animal product consumption.[1] It also reflects my opinion that a vegetarian, whole food, very low-fat diet is generally ideal, especially for those trying to control their weight.

In summary, the body of the pyramid below the dotted line represents foods that promote good health and should be used on a daily basis. The foods above the dotted line are not necessary for good health. Avoid them as much as possible, if you want to make the HawaiiDiet™ work for you.

For those who have health conditions that might affect their digestion, absorption, metabolism or otherwise affect their nutrition, please consult your own physician while making your decision about using or giving up these foods.

If you follow the principles of the HawaiiDiet™, and the HawaiiDiet™ Pyramid properly, you'll have a diet that has the following characteristics.

1. The HawaiiDiet™ Is Centered on Whole Complex Carbohydrates.

One of the key elements of the traditional Hawaiian diet was a strong reliance on whole, complex carbohydrates in the form of whole grains. This is also common to most traditional cultures.

2. The HawaiiDiet™ Is Low In Fat.

Most traditional diets were very low in fat. The range for most traditional cultures is around 6 to 19 percent fat. Consistent with these diets, the HawaiiDiet™ Pyramid produces a very low-fat diet because of its focus on low-fat, whole-plant-based foods. Animal flesh and added fats and oils are virtually or completely eliminated, and fats come from the oils found naturally in the foods. Some individuals may have the genetic makeup to tolerate higher fat diets. However, for those who have a problem with weight, a low-fat diet is ideal based on our research.

3. The HawaiiDiet™ Encourages a No Cholesterol Diet.

Nearly all ancient traditional diets were semi-vegetarian or vegetarian. From the perspective of cholesterol-related disease, a no-cholesterol diet is ideal and, since all dietary cholesterol comes from animal products *(including fish and fowl)*, the ideal diet is vegetarian *(provided it is done properly)*. This is reflected in the HawaiiDiet™ Pyramid. Today, a wealth of research indicates that this is an optimal diet for human weight control and health.

4. The HawaiiDiet™ Is High in Vegetables and Fruits.

All major traditional cultural diets were grain and plant-based. This means that vegetables and fruit were eaten in great abundance. Today, major health organizations now suggest that we eat a minimum of five servings per day of fruits and vegetables, in order to be well nourished. The HawaiiDiet™ makes the best use of these most delicious foods. In the recipe section, you'll find a variety of novel ways to prepare them.

5. The HawaiiDiet™ Is High In Mass Index.

The "SMI" stands for Shintani's Mass Index of Food *(also known as "EMI" for Eat More Index)*. The SMI is a table that describes food based on an "Index" number that helps you evaluate the weight loss effect of foods.

How Much Should I Eat?

With the HawaiiDiet™, you don't have to cheat on portion sizes. You don't even have to consider them. Just make sure that you're eating only approved types of foods. That should be no problem. You'll find plenty of variety in the HawaiiDiet™ Pyramid, and you'll be able to find the food that helps you lose weight by using the SMI. This way of eating offers the best variety, the best flavors, the best textures of any type of food.

The Mass Index of Food: How to Find Foods that Cause Weight Loss

Let me give you an overview of the index I devised to help you examine which foods satisfy you the most per calorie. It is a totally new way of looking at food and is one of the pillars of the diet. The SMI number generally represents the number of pounds of food it takes to provide 2,500 calories, which is one day's worth of calories for an average active woman or average inactive man. For example, the SMI value of corn is 6.5, which means that it takes 6.5 pounds of corn to make your daily 2,500 calories.

The Simple Logic of the SMI

Now, here's the simple logic of the SMI: *the higher the SMI the better.* If average people were to eat just corn for a day *(and I'm not suggesting you do that)*, they would have to eat 6.5 pounds of it to get one day's calorie requirement and maintain their weight *(based on a 2,500-calorie requirement — the actual amount varies from person to person)*. Obviously, average individuals will have great difficulty eating this much corn *(30 ears!)* and will likely eat less than this amount and still be full. Thus, while eating as much as they want, they will still lose weight.

Another example is potatoes. They have an SMI value of 9.6, which means that an average person would have to eat 9.6 pounds to get one day's calories. Again, just about everyone will feel full with less than 9.6 pounds of potatoes *(that's about 24 small potatoes or 12 larger ones)* and thus would lose weight if eating just potatoes. A couple of other examples are broccoli, with an SMI value of 17.1 *(17.1 pounds of broccoli to make one day's calories)*; and apples, with an SMI value of 9.4 *(9.4 pounds of apples to make one day's calories)*, which is equal to about 31 apples! Clearly, the average person is not going to eat enough of any of these individual foods to even maintain their weight. Therefore, any combination of these foods will provide a varied diet that will naturally induce weight loss.

By sharp contrast, foods that are low in SMI can easily produce weight gain. The foods that are lowest in SMI are oils and fats.

Oils and fats have an SMI value of 0.61 *(100% fat)* and can easily be eaten in enough quantity to produce weight gain. Butter and margarine are 0.76 *(99% to 100% fat)*, mayonnaise is 0.78 *(98% fat)*. Such very low SMI foods are what I consider "diet destroyers" and should be avoided or minimized.

In other words, the higher the SMI number of a food *(that is, the more pounds of food it takes to provide your daily calories)*, the more likely you are to be satisfied by eating a selected food. Choosing foods in this way emphasizes the positive aspect and encourages people to "eat more" of these foods, which helps promote automatic weight loss. In this way, the SMI allows you to select foods that will help you lose weight while you eat until you're satisfied. For a full description of the SMI, see my earlier book, *Dr. Shintani's Eat More, Weigh Less* ® *Diet.*

The following is the menu that was used in the "Hawaii Health Program," which is now also known as the "Governor's Diet."

Hawaii Health Program Menu — Week 1

Day		Breakfast
1	This first day of the HawaiiDiet™, we provided a traditional Hawaiian menu for breakfast and dinner and a modern adaptation for lunch. This helped to emphasize that there are Hawaiian concepts behind the program and that the program is not just a "diet" but a whole person, whole community program.	Sweet Potato (*p. 53*), Taro (*p. 55*), Fresh Fruit, Mamaki Tea
2	The second day of the program demonstrated that taro could be used in creative ways as in pancakes. The Governor was featured on TV and in the newspapers eating this lunch. The dinner was a dish designed by Hawaii Regional Cuisine Chef Peter Merriman.	Taro Pancakes with Fruit Topping (*p.60*), Papaya, Mamaki Tea
3	The breakfast on day 3 was designed to reflect a traditional Japanese breakfast that is and has always been low in fat and without cholesterol. The lunch and dinner also reflected an Asian theme.	Breakfast Miso Soup (*p.63*), Basmati Brown Rice (*p.204*) , Fresh Fruit, Green Tea
4	Day 4 provided a simple, modern American healthy breakfast. The lunch and dinner were favorite dishes on the HawaiiDiet™ Study where we compared traditional Mediterranean diet with traditional Asian diet.	Whole Oatmeal with Raisins (*p.57*), Fresh Fruit, Mamaki Tea
5	Day 5 provides a menu that started with a traditional Chinese dish called Congee or popularly known as "Jook," a Chinese rice porridge. The lunch was a simple low-fat dish and the dinner was another traditional Hawaiian meal.	Confetti Congee (*p. 209*), Fresh Fruit, Green Tea
6	Day 6. The breakfast dish "Pho" is Vietnamese noodles. The lunch was highlighted with an East-West creation by Peter Merriman of a cold Gazpacho soup served with a favorite Chinese dish. Dinner was traditional Thai in origin.	Pho (*p. 150*), Basmati Brown Rice (*p.204*), Fresh Fruit, Green Tea
7	On this day, we provided another traditional Hawaiian breakfast. Lunch included "Lomi Tomato" which is a vegetarian version of Lomi Salmon. Dinner was a Hawaiian-Japanese hybrid dish.	Taro (*p. 55*) , Whole Oatmeal with Raisins (*p.57*), Mamaki tea

Lunch	Dinner
Potato and Corn Chowder *(p.77)*, Peter Merriman's Mixed Green Vegetable Salad with Ka`u Gold® Potatoes *(p. 118)*, Maui Onions, Broccoli, Pineapple	Lawalu Chicken *(p. 128)*, Mountain Fern *(Ho`i`o)* Salad *(p. 112)*, Poi, Sweet Potato *(p. 53)*, Taro *(p. 55)*, Fresh Fruit, Mamaki Tea
Tofu Stir Fry *(p. 176)*, Spicy Szechuan Eggplant *(p. 198)*, Basmati Brown Rice *(p.204)*, Fresh Fruit, Mamaki Tea	Peter Merriman's Baked Ono *(p. 139)*, with Black Bean Sauce *(p. 92)*, Basmati Brown Rice *(p.204)*, Wakame Namasu *(p. 192)*, Fresh Fruit, Green Tea
Pan Sushi *(p. 69)*, Mediterranean Musubi *(p. 67)*, Fresh Citrus Salad *(p. 127)*, Green Tea	Shrimp with Snowpeas & Mushrooms *(p. 146)*, Brown Rice *(p. 205)*, Herbed Asparagus *(p. 199)*, Fresh Fruit, Mamaki Tea
Mock Crabmeat Sauce over Broccoli *(p. 194)*, Basmati Brown Rice *(p. 204)*, Fresh Fruit, tea	Peking Hot & Sour Soup *(p. 86)*, Brown Rice *(p. 205)*, Tofu Stir Fry *(p. 176)*, Fresh Fruit, Green Tea
Cold Somen Salad *(p. 109)*, Fresh Fruit, Iced Mamaki Tea	Lawalu Chicken *(p. 128)*, Poi, Sweet Potato *(p. 53)*, Taro *(p. 55)*, Manauwea *(Ogo)* Salad *(p. 111)*, Fresh Fruit, Mamaki Tea
Peter Merriman's Asian Gazpacho *(p. 76)*, Vegetarian Eight Treasures *(p. 169)*, Basmati Brown Rice *(p. 204)*, Fresh Fruit, Iced Tea	Chicken Papaya *(p. 134)*, Miso Potato Salad *(p. 117)*, Green Bean Salad *(p. 124)*, Hot Spiced Apples *(p. 217)*, Mamaki Tea
Thai Vegetable Curry *(p. 173)*, Thai Jasmine Rice *(p. 212)*, Lomi Tomato *(p.121)*, Fresh Fruit, Mamaki Tea	Wakame Soup *(p. 84)*, Taro Hekka *(p. 132)*, Green Salad with Dressing, Brown Rice *(p. 205)* , Fresh Fruit, Tea

Hawaii Health Program Menu — Week 2

Day		Breakfast
8	On day 8, we started with a treat for breakfast and provided a delicious local style lunch and a Korean style dinner.	Banana Crepes with Fruit Topping (p. 58), Fresh Fruit, Tea
9	After another traditional Hawaiian breakfast, we provided a Hawaiian stew for lunch that was so well liked that it has been in the papers and on the "Electric Kitchen". The surprise is that it has no meat in it.	Sweet Potato (p. 53), Taro (p. 55), Fresh Fruit, Mamaki Tea
10	Today's dinner, the mushroom rice, was so popular on the Program and the HawaiiDiet™ Study that we had it at the Governor's reception at the end of the program.	Banana Bread (p. 62), Papaya, Mamaki Tea
11	The lunch for day 11 of this program was a Mark Ellman creation. The Salmon Hot Pot was highly rated by participants but remember to get fresh salmon when you prepare it to make the most of it.	Breakfast Miso Soup (p.63), Basmati Brown Rice (p. 204), Fresh Fruit, Green Tea
12	This day was highlighted by a Peter Merriman "Hula Grill" (Maui) dish, "Ginger-Pineapple Chicken," which he personally served at the Governor's reception. At lunch the menu included a traditional Filipino noodle dish, "Pansit."	Whole Oatmeal with Raisins (p.57), Fresh Fruit, Mamaki Tea
13	The breakfast on this day was a no-cholesterol replacement for scrambled eggs. The lunch was a low-fat version of chili and dinner a creation of Chef Roy Yamaguchi.	Scrambled Tofu (p. 61), Whole Wheat Toast or Brown Rice (p. 205), Fresh Fruit, Mamaki Tea
14	Summer Roll for lunch is a treat and was eventually served at the Governor's reception. It is actually easier to prepare than you might think. The Mustard Cabbage with Konbu is an excellent high-calcium side dish.	Wakame Soup (p. 84), Basmati Brown Rice (p. 204), Fresh Fruit, Tea

Lunch	Dinner
Chicken Broccoli *(p. 135)*, Basmati Brown Rice *(p. 204)*, Sweet Potato *(p. 53)*, Fresh Fruit, Mamaki Tea	Chop Chae *(p. 149)* , Watercress & Bean Sprouts Namul *(p. 114)*, Kim Chee, Fresh Fruit, Tea
Hawaiian Savory Stew *(p. 159)*, Brown Rice *(p. 205)*, Green Salad with Papaya Seed Dressing *(p. 98)*, Fresh Fruit, Tea	Tofu Stir Fry *(p. 176)*, Basmati Brown Rice *(p. 204)*, Lomi Tomato *(p.121)*, Stovetop Malted Pears *(p.220)*, Tea
Lawalu Chicken *(p. 128)*, Brown Rice *(p. 205)*, Fresh Fruit, Herb Tea	Baked Rice with Shiitake Mushrooms *(p. 211)*, Dark Greens Salad with Mark Ellman's Tomato Miso Vinaigrette *(p. 100)*, Kabocha Squash *(p. 200)*, Fresh Fruit, Green Tea
Green Tea Noodles Salad *(p. 108)*, Brown Rice *(p. 205)*, Watercress & Bean Sprout Namul *(p. 114)*, Fresh Fruit, Iced Tea	Salmon Hot Pot *(p. 144)*, Brown Rice *(p. 205)*, Spinach Salad with Tangy Dijon Dressing *(p. 102)*, Fresh Fruit, Mamaki Tea
Noodles With Chicken - Filipino Style *(Pansit) (p. 138)*, Fragrant Salad *(p. 122)*, Fresh Fruit, Iced Herb Tea	Hula Grill's Ginger & Pineapple Chicken *(p.136)*, Brown Rice *(p. 205)*, Watercress/Sweet Potato Leaf Salad *(p. 113)*, Tea
Chunky 2-Bean Chili *(p. 80)*, with Brown Rice *(p. 205)*, Green Salad with Dressing, Fresh Fruit, Iced Tea	Roy's Blackened `Ahi with Soy-Mustard Sauce *(p. 142)*, Roasted Potatoes *(p. 201)*, Herbed Asparagus *(p. 199)*, Fresh Fruit, Herb Tea
Summer Roll with Dipping Sauce *(pp. 64-65)*, Brown Rice *(p. 205)*, Green Papaya Salad *(p. 126)*, Fresh Fruit, Green Tea	Shrimp with Snowpeas, Brown Rice *(p. 205)*, Ginger Mustard Cabbage with Konbu *(p. 193)*, Fruit, Mamaki Tea

Hawaii Health Program Menu — Week 3

Day		Breakfast
15	This was a no cholesterol week. Maui Tacos' Black Bean Burrito made for a yummy lunch. The sweet and sour tofu is a great meatless alternative for this traditional dish.	Sweet Potato (*p. 53*), Taro (*p. 55*), Fresh Fruit, Tea
16	The Portuguese Bean Soup is a local favorite that typically has pork in it. You'll see that it is delicious without pork as well.	Banana Bread (*p. 62*), Fresh Fruit, Herb Tea
17	Vegetarian Eight Treasures is a Chinese dish that includes eight different delicious ingredients. The dinner on this day is a demonstration of a meatless traditional Hawaiian meal.	Confetti Congee (*p. 209*), Fresh Fruit, Green Tea
18	Mu Shu Vegetables is a variation on the Szechwan dish, "Mu Shu Pork." This is a "must-try" dish and was also served at the Governor's reception.	Bagels, Fresh Fruit, Tea
19	Gandule Rice is a surprisingly delicious Puerto Rican one-dish meal. Anyone who likes chili should like this one.	Breakfast Miso Soup (*p.63*), Basmati Brown Rice (*p. 204*), Fresh Fruit, Tea
20	Healthy Manapua is a treat. The "char siu" in this dish is made of wheat gluten. The Pasta Gerry is a Pacific Rim Cuisine creation of Mark Ellman of Avalon.	Scrambled Tofu (*p. 61*), Whole Wheat Toast, Fruit Preserves, Herb Tea
21	The Kabobs are a delicious festive dish and the Quinoa is an exotic light grain that you can find in the health food store. We closed with mushroom rice and the dressing because they were among the group's favorite dishes.	Sweet Potato (*p. 53*), Taro (*p. 55*), Fresh Fruit, Tea

Lunch	Dinner
Maui Tacos Black Bean Burrito *(p. 184)*, Green Salad and Papaya Seed Dressing *(p. 98)*, Fresh Fruit, Tea	Sweet and Sour Tofu with Chinese Peas & Mushrooms *(p. 177)*, Apple Bran Cake *(p. 225)*, Fresh Fruit, Chinese Tea
Portuguese Bean Soup *(p. 79)*, Whole Wheat Bread, Green Salad with Balsamic Vinaigrette *(p. 104)*, Fresh Fruit, Tea	Hawaiian Savory Stew *(p. 159)*, Brown Rice *(p. 205)*, Green Salad with Dressing, Pineapple Sorbet *(p. 238)*, Tea
Vegetable Eight Treasures *(p. 169)*, Basmati Brown Rice *(p. 204)*, Fresh Fruit, Iced Mamaki Tea	Vegetarian Laulau *(p. 164)*, Tofu Poke *(p. 66)*, Manauwea *(Ogo)* Salad *(p. 111)*, Poi, Fresh Fruit, Sweet Potato *(p. 53)*, Mamaki Tea
Soba Salad *(p. 105)*, Fresh Fruit, Green Tea	Mu Shu Vegetables with Chapati *(p. 153)*, String Beans, Fresh Citrus Salad *(p. 127)*,, Tea
Gandule Rice *(p. 207)*, Green Salad with Dressing, Fresh Fruit, Tea	Tofu Stir Fry *(p. 176)*, with Black Bean Sauce *(p. 176)*, Brown Rice *(p. 205)*, Spicy Szechuan Eggplant *(p. 198)*, Lime-Honey Shave Ice *(p. 239)*, Tea
Healthy Char Siu Manapua *(p. 71)*, Summer Relish Salad *(p. 123)*, Fresh Fruit, Tea	Avalon's Pasta Gerry *(p. 181)*, Great Caesar Salad *(p. 115)*, Fresh Fruit, Tea
Kabobs with Marinade *(p. 155)*, Quinoa Pilaf *(p. 213)*, Fresh Fruit, Tea	Baked Rice with Shiitake Mushrooms *(p. 211)*, Dark Greens Salad with Mark Ellman's Tomato Miso Vinaigrette *(p. 100)*, Kabocha Squash *(p. 200)*, Berry Nests *(p. 230)* , Green Tea

Chapter 5
Recipes

Breakfast

This section is called "Breakfast," but some of the items in this section can be used as main staple foods. As you have read, the largest part of the HawaiiDiet™ is a whole starchy staple. In this section, the sweet potato, taro, and oatmeal could also be used as main staples on this diet. Conversely, the brown rice *(page 205)* and also the "Confetti Congee" *(page 209)* found in the "Staples" section were used as breakfast on the HawaiiDiet™.

Sweet Potato ('Uala)

Also known as "'uala" in Hawaiian, sweet potato is an excellent high-bulk, high "SMI" staple that fills you up. It has the versatility of being a dessert as well and is an excellent semisweet snack to curb those cravings for sweets. ❧

2 or 3   Sweet Potatoes
Water

Wash sweet potatoes to clean.

Steamed:

Pour 3/4" to 1" of water into a pot or steamer. Place sweet potatoes on the steamer rack and cover. Steam for 25 to 30 minutes or until fork tender. Portion into 4-ounce servings.

If you have a rice cooker, place about 1" of water in the pot and place the sweet potato on a rack inside the pot. Turn on the rice cooker, and when it turns itself off, the sweet potatoes should be steamed perfectly.

Boiled:

Heat pan to boiling in enough water to cover sweet potatoes. Cover and cook for 30 to 45 minutes or until fork tender. Portion into 4-ounce servings.

Baked:

Wrap in foil for extra moistness or prick with a fork and bake in 350° F. oven for 45 to 60 minutes. Portion into 4-ounce servings. *(1 portion = 118 calories., 0.1 gram fat, 7% protein, 92% carbohydrates, 1% fat)*

Taro *(Kalo)*

Although many people are familiar with poi (the mashed or pounded form of taro), most people are unfamiliar with cooked "table" taro — that is, taro meant to be cooked and eaten in chunks rather than as poi. It is really important to get high quality taro for use as "table" taro; otherwise it is a poor taste choice. My favorite is a type called "moi" and a close second is "lehua" which is the type used to make poi. ॐ

1-2 lbs.   **Taro**
        Water

Wash and scrub taro thoroughly until clean.

Do NOT eat taro or taro leaves raw. Taro must be cooked properly.

> *"Kalo [taro] has a high concentration of calcium oxalate, which are needle-like crystals found throughout the entire plant. Kalo [taro] must be cooked properly. If it is eaten raw or half cooked, it may cause itching in the throat."*[1]

Do not peel the skin off the taro prior to boiling or steaming. It is easier and less itchy to cook unpeeled and peel it after it is cooked.

If your skin gets itchy after contact with raw taro or taro leaves, make a paste out of baking soda and water, then spread on affected area until itching disappears, then wash off.

Steamed:

Place whole taro in a steamer or pressure cooker with water. Steam on high heat for 2 hours or in a pressure cooker for 1 hour. *(See "After Cooking" below.)*

Boiled:

Place scrubbed taro in a large pot. Add water to half cover the whole taro. Cover pot and boil 2 hours or until fork tender. *(See "After Cooking" below.)*

After Cooking:

The taro is fully cooked when fork tender. Cool under cold tap water. Remove outer skin by scraping with a dull knife or spoon. Cut into slices or cubes. Serve warm or cold.

Makes 4 portions. *(1 portion = 161 calories, 0.1 gram fat, 1% protein, 98% carbohydrates, 1% fat)*

Whole Oatmeal

This is a simple breakfast that can be enhanced greatly by pan-roasting the oatmeal before cooking. The Governor apparently found it delicious and his chef liked it so much that he said he once had it for lunch. ☞

1 C	Whole oats
1 tsp.	Vanilla
1 tsp.	Salt
4 C	Water

Bring water to a boil, add oatmeal, whisk until oatmeal is tender but still well defined, about 10 to 15 minutes at medium heat. Drain, scoop into bowls, and serve.

For a toasty flavor, dry roast the oatmeal on a skillet over medium heat until slightly brown before adding the water.

The amount of water used will determine the texture of the oatmeal. For a thicker oatmeal, use less water; for a thinner consistency use more water, to taste.

Makes 4 portions. *(1 portion = 155 calories, 2.7 grams fat, 17% protein, 68% carbohydrates, 15% fat)*

Banana or Blueberry Crepes

Banana Crepes was one of the favorite breakfasts on the Hawaii Health Program. In this recipe, you will notice "egg replacer" which eliminates the cholesterol from this dish. You can use your favorite fruit to wrap in these light crepes. ○3

BATTER:

1/2 C + 1 tsp.	Egg replacer
1 C	Water
1 Tbsp.	Honey substitute *(available at health food stores)* or honey
1 C	Whole wheat pastry flour
2/3 C	Applesauce
1 tsp.	Vanilla extract
	Nonfat cooking spray

FILLING:

3 C	Bananas or blueberries
2 Tbsp.	Honey substitute
few drops	Lemon juice *(fresh)*
	Powdered sugar

Crepes:

In a food processor or blender, combine egg replacer, water, and honey substitute; process until smooth. Beat in flour, applesauce, and vanilla extract and let batter stand for 5 minutes.

Lightly spray skillet with cooking spray. Heat over medium-high heat.

Pour 1/4 cup of batter into hot skillet. Lift skillet off burner and tilt until the batter covers the bottom of the skillet evenly. Return to heat and cook 15 to 20 seconds, until the top is dry and the bottom a golden brown. Flip crepe over and cook the other side. Turn the crepes out onto a dinner plate and repeat procedure until you have used up all the batter.

These can be made ahead of time. Keep them tightly covered and refrigerated. Place the filling in the crepes, cover with aluminum foil, and place in a 325° F. oven.

Filling:

In a saucepan, combine bananas *(or blueberries),* honey substitute or honey, and a few drops of lemon juice. Cook over medium heat for 3 to 5 minutes. Spoon the desired amount of filling into the crepe and roll. Sprinkle with powdered sugar.

This sauce can be made ahead of time. Place it in a tightly covered container and refrigerate.

Makes 6 portions of banana or blueberry crepes. *(1 portion banana crepe = 264 calories, 1.3 grams fat, 6% protein, 90% carbohydrates, 4% fat) . (1 portion blueberry crepe = 191 calories, 1.0 gram fat, 7% protein, 88% carbohydrates, 5% fat)*

Taro Pancakes

This is a great way to use leftover taro. ❧

1-1/4 C	Whole wheat pastry flour
pinch	Salt
1-1/4 C	Rice Dream® or skim milk
1 tsp.	Egg replacer
1/2 C	Water
1 tsp.	Macadamia nut oil or Canola oil
1 C	Taro, cooked, cleaned, and coarsely grated
	(See cooking instructions on page 55.)
1 tsp.	Vanilla
	Pam® No Stick Cooking Spray

Sift flour and salt together. Place in food processor. Mix Rice Dream® or skim milk, egg replacer, water, and oil in a large measuring cup. Add to flour mixture in food processor. Process until smooth. Fold in taro.

Lightly spray skillet with cooking spray. Heat skillet or griddle over medium-high heat. Pour into skillet or griddle 1/4 cup of batter for each pancake and cook. Turn pancake over when bubbles appear and cook until golden brown on both sides.

Serve with guava or passion fruit syrups. *Guava jelly or passion fruit jelly may be placed in a saucepan with water and thinned down to a syrup.*

Makes 8 portions. *(1 portion = 116 calories, 1.9 grams fat, 13% protein, 72% carbohydrates, 14% fat)*

Scrambled Tofu*

Scrambled Tofu is a delicious substitute for scrambled eggs. The best reason to replace eggs for breakfast is the 430 mg. of cholesterol found in two eggs (more than the amount of cholesterol in an 8-ounce steak). Tofu, of course, as in any plant-based product, has no cholesterol. ෬

1 block	Tofu, firm
1/4 C	Onions, minced
2 tsp.	Vegetarian "chicken-flavored" seasoning
1/2 tsp.	Turmeric
1/4 tsp.	Sea salt
1/4 tsp.	Onion powder
1/4 tsp.	Garlic powder
	Canola oil cooking spray

Lightly spray a large nonstick skillet with canola oil cooking spray. Sauté onions, adding a slight amount of water if they start to stick. As the onions cook, add seasonings and mix.

Break up tofu into scrambled-egg consistency and add to the mixture. Cook until the mixture is thoroughly heated and resembles scrambled eggs.

Serve with whole grain toast or pancakes.

Makes 5 portions. *(1 portion = 95 calories, 4.2 grams fat, 38% protein, 24% carbohydrates, 38% fat)*

* From **Dr. Shintani's Eat More, Weigh Less® Cookbook**, page 93

Banana Bread

Banana Bread was another favorite on the Hawaii Health Program . What is unique about this banana bread recipe is that is has much less oil than in most banana bread recipes.

 C&

3 large	Bananas, very ripe and mashed
1/4 C	Egg replacer
2 Tbsp.	Applesauce
1/3 C	Honey substitute or honey
1/4 C	Rice Dream® or skim milk
1/2 tsp.	Salt
1 tsp.	Baking soda
1 tsp.	Baking powder
1-1/2 C	Whole wheat pastry flour
	Nonstick cooking spray

Preheat oven to 350° F.

In a food processor, combine bananas, egg replacer, applesauce, sugar, Rice Dream® or skim milk, and salt. Beat well. Add the baking soda and baking powder. Gently blend in the flour and blend for about 20 seconds or until moistened.

Spray a small loaf pan *(7-1/2" x 3")* with nonstick cooking spray and pour batter into pan. Bake for 45 minutes or until toothpick inserted in the center comes out clean.

Makes 8 portions. *(1 portion = 158 calories, 1.0 gram fat, 11% protein, 84% carbohydrates, 5% fat)*

*Breakfast Miso Soup**

Miso soup for breakfast may sound a little odd, but believe me, on a cold day this is a delicious treat. Miso soup with rice is commonly eaten for breakfast in Japan where their heart disease rates are very low. This low rate of heart disease is partially owing to the fact that miso soup and rice contain no cholesterol. ℃

2-1/2 C	Water
1	Wakame seaweed *(3" strip)*
1/8 C	Tofu *(firm)*, chopped to 1/2" chunks
1	Green onion with stems, chopped fine
1-2 Tbsp.	Barley miso

Bring water to a boil, add wakame and one-half of green onion. Simmer 5 minutes.

Turn off heat, add miso to taste by diluting 1 to 2 tablespoons of miso in a ladle full of soup water, mashing, and smoothing out the miso and adding it back to the pot.

Pour into a large bowl, over small chunks of tofu. Garnish with chopped green onions and serve steaming hot.

Makes 4 to 6 portions. *(1 portion = 18 calories, 0.8 gram fat, 30% protein, 34% carbohydrates, 35% fat)*

* From **Dr. Shintani's Eat More, Weigh Less® Cookbook**, page 178

Appetizers or Snacks

Summer Rolls＊

Summer rolls are a delicious, naturally low-fat, festive food – great for parties and special occasions. ❧

1 pkg.	Rice paper *(10 or 20 sheets)*
1 C	Rice sticks, softened by cooking
1 head	Romaine lettuce
1/8 C	Basil *(fresh) (optional)*
1 C	Mint leaves
1/8 C	Cilantro *(fresh) (optional)*
1 C	Bean sprouts *(fresh)*
1 C	Carrots, shredded
1 C	Tofu *(firm)*, cut into strips

Cook rice sticks according to package instructions. Dip rice papers in water and place on paper towels to allow them to soften.

Place lettuce, rice sticks *(now soft as noodles)* along with other ingredients in a row across the middle of rice paper and roll like a burrito. Place seam side down on serving tray.

Makes 20 portions. See dips, next page. *(1 portion = 131 calories, 1.2 grams fat, 8% protein, 84% carbohydrates, 8% fat)*

＊ From **Dr. Shintani's Eat More, Weigh Less® Cookbook**, page 280

Clear Dip*

2 cloves	Garlic, crushed
6 Tbsp.	Barley malt, rice syrup, or sugar
1 Tbsp.	Lemon juice
1 Tbsp.	Rice vinegar
4 Tbsp.	Water
	Chili *(fresh)*, to taste

Mix ingredients together and use as a dipping sauce. Makes 20 portions to use with summer rolls. *(1 portion = 14 calories, 0 gram fat, 1% protein, 99% carbohydrates, 0% fat)*

Amber Dip*

1 C	Chinese bean sauce
1/4 C	Barley malt, rice syrup, or sugar
2 cloves	Garlic, minced
1/2 C	Water
	Cornstarch, as needed for texture

On medium heat, cook bean sauce, sugar, and garlic together for 3 to 4 minutes, stirring constantly. Add water and stir. Thicken with cornstarch mixed with water, if necessary.

Ground peanuts can also be added as a garnish. Just remember that using a lot of peanuts will increase the fat content of this dish.

Makes 20 portions to be used with summer rolls. *(1 portion = 19 calories, 0.3 gram fat, 12% protein, 73% carbohydrates, 15% fat)   *   From* **Dr. Shintani's Eat More, Weigh Less®** Cookbook*, page 281*

Tofu Poke

Typical "poke" is made with fish, but in order to eliminate the cholesterol we did it with tofu with "broke da mouth" results. ❧

1 block	Tofu *(extra firm)*
2	Green onions, chopped
1	Red chili pepper, chopped
1/2	Sweet round onion, quartered and sliced thin
1/2 C	Ogo *(manauwea)* seaweed, blanched, and chopped
1/2 tsp.	Hawaiian salt
1/2 tsp.	Sesame seed oil

Prepare vegetables prior to mixing.

Slice block of tofu into 1/2" cubes into a bowl. Add green onion, chili pepper, round onion, then seaweed. Sprinkle Hawaiian salt and sesame seed oil.

Toss lightly and let sit for at least 1 hour, then serve.

Makes 6 portions. *(1 portion = 65 calories, 3.6 grams fat, 35% protein, 19% carbohydrates, 45% fat)*

Mediterranean Musubi

Here is a dish where East meets West. ("Musubi" means rice ball.) ଔ

2-3/4 C	Water
2 C	Brown rice
1/2 C	Whole wheat mochi rice
3-4	Umeboshi plums, minced
1 can	Garbanzo beans, drained
2-3 Tbsp.	Furikake
1 head	Romaine lettuce

Soak all rice in cold water for 15 minutes to soften. Wash and drain rice well. Cook in rice cooker or pot. When done, turn off and let stand for 10 minutes.

Place rice into a bowl and allow to cool. Toss in umeboshi plums, garbanzo beans, and furikake. Lay on a boat of romaine lettuce.

To eat, fold the lettuce lengthwise and eat taco fashion.

Makes 9 portions. *(1 portion = 122 calories, 1.6 grams fat, 13% protein, 75% carbohydrates, 11% fat)*

Mediterranean Sushi

Another dish where East meets West. ("Su" in "Sushi" means vinegar, so "Sushi" is rice with vinegar flavor.) ∞

2-1/2 C	Water
2 C	Brown rice
1/2 C	Whole wheat mochi rice
1 can	Garbanzo beans, drained
2-3 Tbsp.	Furikake
1 head	Romaine lettuce

SUSHI FLAVORING:

Heat and cool the following:

1/4 C	Rice vinegar
1/3 C	Sugar or honey
3/4 tsp.	Salt

Follow rice cooking directions from Mediterranean Musubi recipe on previous page.

Remove rice and place into a bowl. While the rice is still hot, sprinkle sushi flavoring by teaspoonsful over the rice. Cool by fanning mixture. Then add the garbanzo beans and furikake.

Serve on romaine lettuce and garnish with additional furikake.

Makes 9 portions. *(1 portion = 143 calories, 1.6 grams fat, 11% protein, 79% carbohydrates, 10% fat)*

Pan Sushi

5 C	Cooked brown rice
1/2 C	Carrots, shredded
1/2 C	Lotus root, shredded
1/2 C	Mushrooms, chopped
1/2 C	Watercress, chopped
1/2 C	Konbu, cooked and chopped

SEASONINGS (or may use packaged sushi mix):

1/4 C	Water
1 Tbsp.	Soy sauce
1 Tbsp.	Mirin
1/2 C	Vinegar
1/2 C	Sugar or honey

Cook brown rice and cool.

Line a 9" x 13" pan with wax paper and set aside.

Sauté vegetables in a skillet adding the water, soy sauce, and mirin. In a bowl, mix brown rice with vinegar and sugar.

Layer half the rice into the lined pan, then layer half the vegetables over the rice. Layer the remaining rice and sprinkle with the remaining vegetables. Cover with wax paper. Using another pan or cutting board, press rice to firm.

Makes 9 portions. *(1 portion = 172 calories, 1.0 gram fat, 7% protein, 86% carbohydrates, 5% fat)*

Manapua

Manapua is a Hawaiian word for what the Chinese call "bao". It is usually filled with seasoned and red-colored (high fat) pork. Here, instead, are some manapua recipes with delicious low-fat, no-cholesterol fillings. ❧

1 pkg. **Bridgeford's® Whole Wheat Frozen Dough, thawed**
Vegetable oil cooking spray

Divide the dough into 12 pieces. Flatten each piece into 4" patties. Place 1-1/2 tablespoons of the filling in the center of the patty. Pull the edges toward the center to seal.

Spray cookie sheet with nonstick spray. Place rolls on the sheet 2" to 3" apart. Follow the package directions for quick rise method. Preheat oven to 350° F. and bake for 25 to 30 minutes. Remove immediately from oven to cool.

To steam, spray bottom of the steamer rack with nonstick spray. Steam for 15 minutes.

This is the basic recipe for Manapua. Be creative and try some different fillings. Here are some of my favorites.

Healthy Char Siu Manapua

6-8 pieces	Seitan, minced
4-5 Tbsp.	Char siu sauce
11-12	Water chestnuts, minced
10-11	Button mushrooms, minced
2	Green onions, thinly sliced

Marinate the seitan in char siu sauce for 1 hour. Water-sauté water chestnuts and mushrooms, then add marinated seitan and green onions.

Place filling into manapua as instructed in manapua dough recipe and cook as directed.

Makes 12 portions. *(1 portion = 393 calories, 5.5 grams fat, 42% protein, 46% carbohydrates, 12% fat)*

Hurry Curry Manapua

5-6 pieces	Seitan, minced
4 Tbsp.	Lee Kum Kee® Vegetarian Stir Fry Sauce
9	Water chestnuts, minced
8	Button mushrooms, minced
2	Green onions, thinly sliced
1-1/2 Tbsp.	Curry powder

Marinate the seitan in the Lee Kum Kee™ sauce for 1 hour. Water-sauté water chestnuts and mushrooms, then add marinated seitan, green onions, and curry powder.

Place filling into manapua as instructed in manapua dough recipe and cook as directed.

Quick An Manapua

1 can   Koshi An *(sweetened azuki beans)*

Use Koshi An to fill the manapua. Place filling into manapua as instructed in manapua dough recipe and cook as directed.

Sweet Potato Manapua

4   Sweet potatoes *(Okinawan or regular),* cooked
     Rice Dream® or skim milk

Mash sweet potato with enough rice or skim milk to give "mashed potato" consistency.

Place filling into manapua as instructed in manapua dough recipe and cook as directed.

Pot Stickers

This is another excellent party favorite. Typical pot stickers are laden with pork, fat, and oil. This version has most of the fat and all of the cholesterol removed. And the sauce makes it lip-smacking good. ଔ

3/4 lb.	Won bok, blanched
8 oz.	Tofu *(firm, frozen)*,thawed
2 tsp.	Cornstarch
1 tsp.	Sesame oil
1/2 tsp.	Salt
1 Tbsp.	Sherry
1 Tbsp.	Tamari or soy sauce
1/4 C	Green onions, minced
1/4 C	Chinese parsley, minced
3 cloves	Garlic, finely minced or pressed
1 pkg.	Mun doo/gyoza wrappers *(12 oz.)*
1 C	Vegetable broth *(more if needed)*
	Vegetable oil cooking spray

DIPPING SAUCE:

2 Tbsp.	Tamari or soy sauce
1 Tbsp.	Rice vinegar
1/2 tsp.	Sesame oil

Chop the won bok very fine; squeeze and drain.

Press tofu to remove excess liquid and cut or break tofu into 1/2" pieces. In a bowl, combine won bok with all ingredients except mun doo wrappers and broth.

Put 1 tablespoon of filling in the center of each wrapper. Dampen edges slightly with water, fold in half, and seal edges by forming 2 to 3 pleats on each side and pinch them to meet the opposite side or use a gyoza press to seal.

Heat oil-sprayed, nonstick skillet over medium-high heat. Arrange dumplings in skillet; cook until bottoms are brown.

Pour in 1/2 cup vegetable broth and cover immediately. Cook on low heat for about 10 minutes or until most of the liquid is absorbed. Check after 5 or 6 minutes. Add 1 to 2 tablespoons more broth or water if liquid dries out too quickly. Uncover and continue cooking until liquid is completely absorbed.

Repeat until all dumplings are cooked.

Serve with dipping sauce *(optional)*.

Makes 6 portions. *(1 portion (2 pot stickers) = 113 calories, 3.6 grams fat, 20% protein, 51% carbohydrates, 27% fat)*

Soups

Presto Minestrone

This is a delightful soup used on the "Mediterranean Diet" tested in the HawaiiDiet™ Study. ℞

4 cloves	Garlic, minced
1	Onion, minced
1	Carrot, cut into 1/2" slices
1 stalk	Celery
1	Potato, cut into 1/2" pieces
1 C	Peas, frozen
2 cans	Italian stewed tomatoes
2 cans	Water
1/2 C	Whole wheat elbow macaroni

Sauté garlic and onions in 2 to 4 tablespoons of water. Add remaining ingredients and simmer for 30 minutes. Add macaroni and boil until macaroni is tender, about 10 minutes.

Makes 8 portions *(8 cups).* *(1 portion = 97 calories, 0.4 gram fat, 14% protein, 82% carbohydrates, 4% fat)*

Peter Merriman's Asian Gazpacho

Asian Gazpacho is a zesty cold soup with an international flavor — great on hot days. ◌ঽ

1/2	Maui onion, peeled
5	Plum tomato, seeded
1	Cucumber, peeled and seeded
1 Tbsp.	Garlic, chopped
1 Tbsp.	Ginger, grated
1	Green bell pepper, seeds and membrane removed
1/4 tsp.	Tabasco® sauce
1/4 C	Rice wine vinegar
1 Tbsp.	Soy sauce
1 C	Tomato juice
1/2 C	Chicken stock
	Chinese parsley, whole leaves *(garnish)*

Pureé first 9 ingredients in food processor until smooth. Add tomato juice and chicken stock and pureé 1 minute longer. Chill until ready to serve. Garnish with Chinese parsley leaves.

Makes 6 portions. *(1 portion = 39 calories, 0.4 gram fat, 18% protein, 74% carbohydrates, 8% fat)*

Potato and Corn Chowder*

Probably the best liked soup on the Hawaii Health Program.
ⓒ

2 tsp.	Dry cooking sherry
1-1/4 C	Sweet yellow onion, finely chopped
2 cloves	Garlic, crushed
2 C	Red potatoes, cubed
1 can	Vegetable stock *(14-1/4 oz.)*
1 C	Soy milk
1 C	Corn kernels *(fresh or frozen)*
1	Bay leaf
1/4 tsp.	Paprika
1/4 tsp.	Thyme
1 tsp.	Basil
	Salt, to taste
	Pepper, to taste
	Olive oil cooking spray

Add wine to a large oil-sprayed skillet and heat. Add onions and garlic and sauté for 5 minutes, stirring frequently to prevent browning. Add water as needed.

Add potatoes, bay leaf, herbs, and stock to sautéed onions and garlic. Cover pan, bring to a boil, and cook over medium heat for 10 to 15 minutes.

When the potatoes are tender, add the corn and milk. Simmer until the corn is tender, about 3 minutes. Discard the bay leaf.

Use your hand blender to partially purée the mixture, or remove a cup of soup and purée in blender or food processor, then return it to the pot. This will give your soup a creamy texture. Season with salt and/or pepper to taste.

Makes 6 to 8 portions.   *(1 portion = 117 calories, 1.3 grams fat, 18% protein, 70% carbohydrates, 10% fat)*

This and other cream soups are a snap to make if you have a hand blender. With this, you can partially blend the soup right in the pot. Just wait until it's almost done then do your blending, leaving enough chunky ingredients to give the soup texture. Watch out for spattering though, if it's really hot.

* From **Dr. Shintani's Eat More, Weigh Less® Cookbook**, page 172

*Portuguese Bean Soup**

This version of a traditional Portuguese favorite is low-fat, no cholesterol, and full-flavored despite the absence of meat. The flavor is retained because of the use of spices. ❧

6 cloves	Garlic, crushed
1-1/2	Round onions, chopped
2 stalks	Celery, chopped
4	Carrots, diced
1 can	Vegetable broth *(14-1/2 oz.)*
2 cans	Whole tomatoes plus juice *(large)*, cut in chunks
3	Potatoes, cubed
3 C	Beans, cooked
1/2 head	Cabbage, chopped
1 C	Macaroni, cooked

Sauté garlic and onions in 2 cups water until transparent. Add celery and carrots. Continue cooking 5 minutes. Add tomatoes and vegetable broth. Add 2 cups more water to mixture. Cook 15 minutes, then add remainder of ingredients, except beans and macaroni. Continue to cook 30 minutes on warm setting, after bringing to a boil. Add beans and simmer on warm for 30 minutes, until done to taste. Add cooked macaroni a few minutes before serving.

Makes 8 portions. *(1 portion = 231 calories, 1.0 gram fat, 20% protein, 76% carbohydrates, 4% fat)*

* From **Dr. Shintani's Eat More, Weigh Less® Cookbook**, page 180

Chunky 2-Bean Chili

Although chili with rice is a favorite in Hawaii, there are many ways to make it (see "Zip Chili" in the Dr. Shintani's Eat More, Weigh Less® Cookbook, page 321). At one of our cooking sessions, this was the favorite recipe. ❧

1/3 C	Vegetable broth
1 C	TVP *(textured vegetable protein)*
3 cloves	Garlic, chopped
1/2	Onion, chopped
1 stalk	Celery, chopped
1	Green pepper, chopped
1 sprig	Cilantro *(Chinese parsley)*, chopped
1-2 Tbsp.	Chili powder
1/2 tsp.	Red pepper flakes
1 tsp.	Cumin
	Black pepper, to taste
2 C	Black beans, *(cooked or canned)*, drained or rinsed
2 C	Kidney beans, *(cooked or canned)*, drained or rinsed
2	Bay leaves
1 C	Tomato sauce
1/2 C	Tomato paste
1/2 C	Water
1 tsp.	Lime juice

Soak the TVP in the broth.

Sauté garlic, onion, celery, green pepper, and cilantro in some vegetable broth. Add the soaked TVP and

remaining ingredients to the mixture and simmer. Adjust seasonings to taste. Remove bay leaves before serving.
Make the day before for better flavor.

Makes 8 portions. *(1 portion = 186 calories, 0.9 gram fat, 39% protein, 57% carbohydrates, 4% fat)*

Corn Soup

This corn soup is especially delicious and a variation of it was served at one of the follow-up sessions of the Governor's group. People liked it so much that they were getting seconds from the kitchen before it ran out. ∞

6 ears	Corn *(fresh)*, husked, silk removed or substitute two packages cut corn *(10 oz., frozen)*, thawed
1 Tbsp.	Water
2 medium	Tomatoes, peeled, and coarsely chopped
1 medium	Onion, finely chopped
1 Tbsp.	Cumin, ground
3 cloves	Garlic, peeled and minced
1	Green pepper, seeds reserved, deribbed, and cubed
1	Red pepper, seeds reserved, deribbed, and cubed
1 tsp.	Lite Salt® *(optional)*
4 cups	Vegetable broth

GARNISH:

Jalapeño pepper, seeded and minced
Cilantro *(fresh)*
Strips of roasted pimento

Cut the kernels from the ears of corn over a bowl to catch any corn milk. Then scrape the ears with the back of a knife to extract the remaining milk. The milk will act as a natural thickener for the soup.

Heat the water in a heavy casserole over low heat. Add the tomato, onion, and cumin. Cook, stirring, until the onion is softened, but not brown. Add the garlic and stir for about 2 minutes. Add the peppers and optional Lite Salt®. Continue stirring until the peppers are slightly limp. Add the stock and corn milk and, stirring, bring to a simmer. Cook 5 minutes, so the corn is still crunchy. Taste for seasonings.

To finish, garnish with cilantro leaves, strips of pimento, and a sprinkle of Jalapeño pepper. For a thicker consistency, thicken with cornstarch and water. Serve hot.

Makes 8 servings. *(1 portion = 106 calories, 1.1 grams fat, 17% protein, 74% carbohydrates, 9% fat)*

Wakame Soup

3 C	Water
2 cloves	Garlic, sliced
1 medium	Onion, chopped
1 medium	Carrot, chopped fine
1 medium	Potato, chopped fine
1 oz.	Wakame *(fresh)*, wash and chop into small pieces
4"x4"	Konbo *(seaweed)*, soaked
3	Shiitake mushroom

In a saucepan, soak konbo and shiitake mushrooms in 3 cups of cold water for 1/2 hour to make broth. Add garlic, onion, carrot, potato, and wakame to the broth and boil.

Makes 6 portions. *(1 portion = 39 calories, 0.2 gram fat, 11% protein, 85% carbohydrates, 4% fat)*

Wakame Onion Mushroom Soup*

1 handful Wakame
1   Onion, diced
4 C   Water
1-2 Tbsp. Miso
2   Shiitake mushrooms *(dried)*

Soak wakame and mushrooms in 1 cup of water until soft, cut into 1" pieces.

Sauté onions in 1/4 cup of water. Add water from soaked wakame and mushrooms and the rest of the water. Bring to a boil, add the wakame and mushrooms, and cook over low flame until it is tender.

Add miso to taste by diluting 1 to 2 tablespoons of miso in a ladle full of the soup water, mashing and smoothing out the miso and adding it back to the pot. Leftover grain or noodles may be added if desired.

Makes 6 portions. *(1 portion = 23 calories, 0.3 grams fat, 16% protein, 73% carbohydrates, 12% fat)*

Variations:

Other variations on this soup would include adding onions, cauliflower, shiitake mushrooms, celery, tofu chunks, etc., to wakame broth. You can also add medium grain brown rice, or barley, or use miso soup as a broth to pour over your whole grains.

* *From **Dr. Shintani's Eat More, Weigh Less**® Cookbook, page 179*

Peking Hot & Sour Soup

2 tsp.	Cornstarch
2 Tbsp.	Cider vinegar
1 can	Vegetable broth with 1-1/2 cup water
1 Tbsp.	Soy sauce *(low sodium)*
1/2 C	Water
1/2 tsp.	Sea salt
1/4 C	Wood ears *(dried black fungus)*
1/4 C	Golden needles *(dried lily flowers)*
1/4 C	Tofu, cubed *(about 1/2 small cake)*
1/4 tsp.	White ground pepper
1 Tbsp.	Scallions, minced *(garnish)*

Boil water and soak wood ears and golden needles separately for about 15 minutes. Break off hard pieces from wood ears and hard stems from golden needles, if any. Cut golden needles in halves and snap the large pieces of wood ears into smaller pieces. Wash and drain.

Mix the cornstarch with 1/2 cup cold water. Stir until smooth.

Mix vinegar and pepper.

Mix vegetable broth and water. Add salt and soy sauce. Bring to a boil and add wood ears and golden needles. Boil 1 minute. Add tofu.

As soup boils, stir in the well-stirred cornstarch mixture until it thickens. Serve in bowl with vinegar and pepper. Garnish with scallions. Serve Hot.

Makes 4 to 6 portions. *(1 portion = 47 calories, 1.2 grams fat, 30% protein, 48% carbohydrates, 21% fat)*

* *From* **Dr. Shintani's Eat More, Weigh Less® Cookbook**, *page 185*

Wheat Berry Vegetable Soup

1 C	Kidney beans *(dried)*, soaked overnight in water and drained
2 tsp.	Olive oil
1 large	Onion, chopped
1 large	Leek, washed well and chopped
1 stalk	Celery, chopped
1 C	Wheat berries, soaked overnight in water and drained
1 medium	Potato, peeled and diced
1-1/2 C	Tomatoes *(canned)*, chopped
3 sprigs	Rosemary *(fresh)*, about 3" long, tied in cheesecloth

Bring beans and 3 cups water to a boil in a medium, covered saucepan. Lower heat and simmer until beans are tender, about 40 minutes to 1 hour.

Heat oil in a separate large saucepan over medium-high heat. Reduce heat to medium-low and add onion, leek, and celery. Sauté, stirring often until soft, about 10 minutes. Stir in beans and cooking water. Add wheat berries, potato, tomato, and rosemary sprigs. Cover and simmer gently over low heat until wheat berries are swollen and tender *(about 40 minutes)*. Stir occasionally to keep vegetables from sticking. Remove rosemary and discard. *Good hot or cold. Freezes well.*

Makes 6 portions. *(1 portion = 224 calories, 2.5 grams fat, 16% protein, 75% carbohydrates, 9% fat)*

Mushroom-Broccoli Noodle Soup*

1 medium	Onion, cut into thin crescents
2 oz.	Mushrooms *(dried)*, soaked and sliced
1 medium	Broccoli bunch, stem cut in quarter rounds and flowerettes cut into 2" pieces
1 can	Water chestnuts, sliced *(8 oz., 5 oz. drained)*,
6 C	Water, boiling
2 C	Vegetable broth
1/4 tsp.	Sea salt
2 C	Soba noodles
2 Tbsp.	Sesame seeds, lightly toasted
2-3 Tbsp.	Soy sauce or tamari *(low sodium)*

In a skillet, water sauté onions until transparent. If they begin to stick, add more water, as necessary.

Add broccoli stems, sauté briefly, then add mushrooms, water chestnuts, boiling water, vegetable broth, and sea salt. Cover and bring to a boil, then lower heat and simmer for 10 minutes.

Add noodles and simmer for a few minutes, until tender. Add broccoli flowerettes, cook until bright green, about 1 minute. Sprinkle sesame seeds onto soup broth. Add soy sauce. Stir and heat, without boiling, until done to taste.

Makes 10 portions. *(1 portion = 78 calories, 1.1 grams fat, 20% protein, 68% carbohydrates, 12% fat)*

* From **Dr. Shintani's Eat More, Weigh Less® Cookbook**, page 169

Condiments and Sauces

Chili Pepper Water

Use to zip your favorite dishes such as the Hawaiian Stew, Tofu Poke, or Chickenless Long Rice. ❦

1/2 C	Hawaiian chilies
1 Tbsp.	Sugar
2 Tbsp.	Hawaiian salt
7 cloves	Garlic
2" piece	Ginger *(fresh)*, peeled

Chop ginger. Stem chilies. Blend all the above ingredients together until smooth. Dilute with water as desired. *Very hot, so use with caution!*

Makes 16 portions. *(1 portion = 8 calories, 0.0 gram fat, 10% protein, 87% carbohydrates, 3% fat)*

Thai Dipping Sauce

This is a great dip for Summer Rolls and Pot Stickers, or as a condiment for Green Papaya Salad. ∞

1/4 C	Sugar
1/2 C	Water
1/2 C	Red wine vinegar
1-2 Tbsp.	Fish sauce or 1/2 to 1 tsp. salt
2 or 3 tsp.	Red chili peppers, ground
1/2	Carrot or daikon, shredded
1/4 C	Peanuts or macadamia nuts, coarsely chopped

In a small saucepan, combine sugar and water. Bring to a boil. Reduce heat and simmer for about 10 minutes or until sugar is dissolved. Remove from heat.

Stir in red wine vinegar, fish sauce, and red chili peppers. Pour sauce into serving bowl. Chill, then top with carrots and sprinkle with nuts before serving.

Makes 2 cups. *(1 portion (1 Tbsp.) = 13 calories, 0.6 gram fat, 9% protein, 56% carbohydrates, 35% fat)*

Peter Merriman's Black Bean Sauce

Use this sauce to add spice to broiled fish or chicken. Or, jazz up a veggie stir fry by adding in the last minute of cooking. ໑

1/2 C	Chinese fermented black beans
1/2 C	Sugar
3/8 C	Soy sauce
1/4 C	Aji Mirin® *(sweet cooking wine)*
2 Tbsp.	Garlic, minced
1-1/2 Tbsp.	Ginger, grated

Wash black beans thoroughly. Place beans into a pot and add enough water to cover 1/2" above the beans.

Combine sugar, soy sauce, mirin, garlic, and ginger. Add this mixture to the beans and water. Bring to a boil and reduce the heat. Cook for 5 minutes. Remove half of this boiled mixture and purée. Place the purée back into the sauce.

Makes 15 portions. *(1 portion = 42 calories, 0.1 gram fat, 12% protein, 87% carbohydrates, 1% fat)*

Lemonnaise

Regular mayonnaise has about 11 grams of fat per table-spoon, and about 99% calories by fat. Eliminate the source of one of the "hidden fats" that put on weight by using this low-fat alternative in salad dressings or as a substitute for mayonnaise. ∝

3 Tbsp.	White vinegar *(distilled)*
1 tsp.	Black peppercorn *(optional)*
1/4 C	Silken tofu
2 Tbsp.	Lemon juice
1 tsp.	Vegetable oil
1/2 tsp.	Dry mustard
	Salt, to taste
	Pepper, to taste

Mix and blend all ingredients in blender. Add salt and pepper at the end of blending to taste.

Makes 10 *(1 tablespoon)* portions. *(1 portion = 10 calories, 0.7 gram fat, 18% protein, 27% carbohydrates, 56% fat)*

Variations:

Aioli – Add 1 clove of minced garlic.

Oriental –Use 2 teaspoons sesame oil instead of vegetable oil.

Chili - Cilantro –Use 4 teaspoons of lime juice instead of lemon juice. Add 1/2 stemmed, fresh *serrano* chili and 1/3 cup freshly chopped cilantro.

Green Sauce – Add 1/2 cup watercress, 1/2 cup green onion, and 1/4 cup parsley.

Tomato Mint Salsa

For a fresh twist, serve this salsa with baked potatoes, pita chips, or as a condiment over fresh vegetables. ❧

1 lb.	Tomatoes *(vine ripened)*
1 C	Green onions, chopped
1/3 C	Basil, chopped
1/3 C	Mint *(fresh)*
3 cloves	Garlic, minced
3 Tbsp.	Lime juice
2 Tbsp.	Soy sauce
2 Tbsp.	Orange juice *(frozen concentrated)*
1-2 tsp.	Chinese chili sauce

Cut tomatoes and squeeze out seeds. Chop either with knife or food processor. Chop green onions, basil, mint, and cilantro. Combine with remaining ingredients.

Do not refrigerate if you are going to serve the same day. If refrigerated, bring to room temperature before serving.

Makes 8 portions. *(1 portion = 27 calories, 0.2 gram fat, 19% protein, 75% carbohydrates, 6% fat)*

Fruit Salsa

2 Tbsp.	Green onion, minced
2 Tbsp.	Cilantro, minced
1 Tbsp.	Ginger *(fresh)*, finely minced
3 Tbsp.	Lime juice, fresh squeezed
2 Tbsp.	Fish sauce
1 tsp.	Chinese chili sauce
2 small	Mangos *(ripe)* or 1 papaya *(ripe)*
	Brown sugar *(optional)*

Using a small bowl, combine green onions, cilantro, ginger, lime juice, fish sauce, and chili sauce.

Peel the mango and chop finely. If using papaya, peel and remove seeds before chopping. Add fruit to mixture. Add brown sugar to taste if desired. Refrigerate.

Makes 4 portions *(2 cups)*. *(1 portion = 85 calories, 0.7 gram fat, 9% protein, 85% carbohydrates, 7% fat)*

Maui Tacos' Pineapple Tomatillo Salsa

This recipe from Mark Ellman's Maui Tacos Restaurant is a flavorful salsa to use in Maui Tacos' Black Bean Burritos. Also, for a tasty snack, try this salsa with your favorite low-fat tortilla chip. Mark Ellman sells this and other delightful salsas in bottles at his restaurants. (Oahu 808-667-5559)

A tomatillo is a savory Mexican vegetable that resembles a small, firm, green tomato with a unique flavor unlike a regular tomato. They are commonly available at Mexican groceries (on Oahu, try Mercado de La Raza at 1315 South Beretania Street). ∾

24 oz.	Pineapple, crushed or 1 whole pineapple *(fresh)*
12 oz.	Tomatillo *(canned)*
2	Jalapeño peppers
1 Tbsp.	Cilantro
1/4	Onion, sliced
3 cloves	Garlic
3 C	Water
1 Tbsp.	Salt

Combine above ingredients in a blender and blend to desired consistency. Refrigerate.

Makes 32 portions *(8 cups).* *(1 portion = 14 calories, 0.1 gram fat, 6% protein, 87% carbohydrates, 7% fat)*

Maui Tacos' Guacamole

Use this guacamole in the Maui Tacos' Black Bean Burrito recipe. Avocados are high in fat, even though it is a better fat than animal fat, so enjoy this delicious condiment in moderation. And if you have trouble losing weight, it's best to avoid avocados in the first place. ∾

2	Avocados, pitted and scooped out *(1/2 lb. avocado pulp)*
2 Tbsp.	Cilantro, finely chopped
3 Tbsp.	Onion, finely chopped
2 tsp.	Lime juice
1 tsp.	Salt
1 tsp.	Jalapeño juice *(no chilies)*
1	Tomato, finely diced

Mash avocados to chunky consistency. Add cilantro, onion, lime juice, and jalapeño juice. Adjust salt to taste. Gently stir in tomatoes to mixture.

Makes 8 *(2-ounce)* portions. *(1 portion = 55 calories, 4.9 grams fat, 5% protein, 21% carbohydrates, 74% fat)*

A word to the wise: Store-bought avocados usually need two or three days to ripen before they are ready to be eaten, so this is a dish you will want to plan in advance.

Salad Dressings

*Papaya Seed Dressing**

1	Papaya *(ripe)*
	Seeds of 1/3 papaya
1 Tbsp.	Dijon mustard
2-3 Tbsp.	Balsamic or red wine vinegar
1 Tbsp.	Soy sauce

Slice one ripe papaya in half, discarding all but 1/3 of the seeds. Scoop out flesh of the papaya and put into blender. Add in the rest of the ingredients and blend on high until smooth.

Makes 10 portions *(about 1+ cups)*. *(1 portion = 8 calories, 0.0 gram fat, 12% protein, 82% carbohydrates, 5% fat)*

* *From Dick Algire in* **Dr. Shintani's Eat More, Weigh Less® Cookbook**, *page 198*

Pineapple Miso Dressing

2 C	Pineapple juice, unsweetened
1/2 C	White miso
1 medium	Maui onion *(mild, sweet onion)*, chopped
2 Tbsp.	Ginger, peeled and minced
1/4 C	Soy sauce, or to taste
1 Tbsp.	Balsamic vinegar *(for fragrance)*
	White pepper, to taste

Blend all the above ingredients together.

Variation:

Substitute pineapple juice with fresh papaya, mandarin oranges, or canned fruit juice.

Makes 24 portions *(about 4 cups)*. *(1 portion = 28 calories, 0.4 grams fat, 15% protein, 73% carbohydrates, 12% fat)*

Mark Ellman's Tomato Miso Vinaigrette

Tomato miso vinaigrette was probably the favorite dressing on the Hawaii Health Program. You will enjoy the Pacific Rim tastes of this dressing, too. ଔ

2 Tbsp.	Onion, chopped
1 C	White wine
1/2 tsp.	Garlic, chopped
2 sprigs	Tarragon *(fresh)*
1 C	Rice vinegar
1 C	Tomato pureé
8 Tbsp.	Red miso
1 tsp.	Sesame seed oil
3 tsp.	Extra virgin olive oil

Sauté onion and garlic in wine. Reduce to a glacé. Add vinegar and reduce by one-half. Add tomato and tarragon. Reduce by one-half and add red miso. Boil once. Emulsify in blender with olive oil and fresh tarragon, with a touch of sesame seed oil. Add water if too thick.

Makes 24 portions. *(1 portion = 31 calories, 1.1 grams fat, 14% protein, 49% carbohydrates, 37% fat)*

*Thousand Island Dressing**

No, this is not the usual high fat version! This one is so good that many people believe that it is "illegal," but when you see that the fat content is less than one gram per serving you'll want to use it more often. ❧

1/4 C	Water
1/8 tsp.	Salt
1/8 tsp.	Pepper
1 tsp.	Seasoned salt
2 Tbsp.	Tomato ketchup
1 C	Tofu *(soft)*, crumbled
4 sprigs	Parsley *(fresh) (optional)*
1 Tbsp.	Cucumber, chopped fine.
1 Tbsp.	Celery, chopped fine

Whiz all ingredients, except cucumber and celery, in blender. Add cucumber and celery. Chill and serve.

Makes 12 portions *(about 1-1/2 cups)*. (1 portion = 18 calories, 0.8 gram fat, 34% protein, 26% carbohydrates, 40% fat)

* From **Dr. Shintani's Eat More, Weigh Less® Cookbook**, page 194

Tangy Dijon Dressing

Even the most finicky eaters will come back for more of this delicious salad dressing. ❧

1 Tbsp.	Canola oil
2/3 C	Water
4-1/2 Tbsp.	White wine vinegar
2-3 cloves	Garlic, minced
4 tsp.	Dijon mustard
1/4 tsp.	Thyme
1/2 tsp.	Salt
1/4 tsp.	Pepper
2 tsp.	Sugar or honey

Mix all ingredients, store in a container, and refrigerate.

Makes 8 portions. *(1 portion = 24 calories, 1.8 grams fat, 2% protein, 31% carbohydrates, 67% fat)*

Oriental Vinaigrette Dressing

For an Oriental flair, add this dressing to vegetables such as won bok, water chestnuts, bean sprouts, or jicama. ♋

4 Tbsp.	Vinegar
4 Tbsp.	Soy sauce
2 Tbsp.	Water
1 tsp.	Sesame oil
1 tsp.	Olive oil
1 Tbsp.	Mustard
2 Tbsp.	Sugar or honey

Combine all ingredients and refrigerate.

Makes 6 portions. *(1 portion = 39 calories, 1.6 grams fat, 11% protein, 55% carbohydrates, 34% fat)*

Balsamic Vinaigrette

The secret ingredient to this dressing is the balsamic vinegar. It is great as a dressing ingredient because like all vinegars it has no fat or cholesterol, and it has a savory, tangy taste without the sour smell of some vinegars. ❧

1/3 C	Balsamic vinegar
1/4 C	Apple cider vinegar
1/4 C	Water
1 Tbsp.	Dijon mustard
1 Tbsp.	Garlic *(fresh)*, minced
1 Tbsp.	Olive oil
1 Tbsp.	Parsley *(fresh)*, minced
2 Tbsp.	Apple juice concentrate

Place ingredients in a small bowl. Whisk together and let sit for at least 15 minutes to allow flavors to meld. Toss with your favorite green salad or pasta salad.

Makes 8 portions. *(1 portion = 25 calories, 1.7 grams fat, 1% protein, 43% carbohydrates, 56% fat)*

Salads

Soba Salad

Soba is a buckwheat noodle and is my favorite noodle because it is made from a whole grain. Soba Salad is an excellent low-fat dish. ଔ

10 oz.	Soba noodles
Water	To cover noodles and to cool noodles while cooking
1 tsp.	Sesame oil
1 Tbsp.	Ginger *(fresh)*, grated
1 Tbsp.	Soy sauce
1/2 C	Broccoli flowerettes, cleaned and chopped into small pieces
1/2 C	Green peas
1/2 C	Soy beans, cooked and drained

In a pot, boil enough water to immerse noodles and place the noodles in the boiling water. As it boils, noodles will foam. Before it overflows, pour a small amount of cool water into the saucepan. *(You will have to do this about three times before it's cooked.)*

If the noodles already contain salt, do not salt the cooking water. If they do not contain salt, a pinch of sea salt can be added to the cooking water.

After the noodles are cooked, drain and rinse in cool water and drain again. Add sesame oil, toss, and refrigerate until cold.

In a large bowl or pan, combine noodles, grated fresh ginger and soy sauce. Add vegetables and soybeans, toss and serve.

Makes 4 portions *(8 ounces of noodles and 1/2 cup of vegetables per serving).* *(1 portion = 304 calories, 3.2 grams fat, 18% protein, 73% carbohydrates, 9% fat)*

Soba with Soy Dressing

6 oz.	Soba noodles
Water	To cover noodles and to cool noodles while cooking
1/2	Carrot, julienned
3 oz.	Shiitake mushrooms

DRESSING:

1 C	Soy sauce
1/4 C	Sushi vinegar
1/4 C	Honey
2 Tbsp.	Ginger *(fresh)*, grated *(use juice only for milder taste)*
2 Tbsp.	Sugar
1 tsp.	Sesame oil

Soak shiitake mushrooms in water until soft. Boil soba noodles until tender. Cool noodles and toss in carrots and shiitake mushrooms. Whisk ingredients for dressing and gently stir into noodle mixture. Serve immediately.

Makes 4 portions. *(1 portion = 284 calories, 1.7 grams fat, 17% protein, 78% carbohydrates, 5% fat)*

Green Tea Noodles Salad

Green Tea Noodle Salad is a creation of Mark Ellman of Avalon Restaurant. The roasted vegetables are a delight. This was served as a lunch on the Hawaii Health Program, and even if you can't get "green tea noodles," it can be done deliciously with other noodles. ☙

2 oz.	Green tea noodles, cooked
2 oz.	Mix grill vegetables *(Brunoise): eggplant, zucchini, mushrooms*
	Salt and pepper to taste
1 oz.	Mark Ellman's Tomato Miso Vinaigrette *(page 100)*
1/3 tsp.	Garlic Mist®

GARNISH:

	Opal basil
2	Tomato quarters, roasted
1	Red romaine leaf

Spray eggplant, zucchini, and mushrooms with Garlic Mist®. Salt and pepper to taste. Grill vegetables until golden brown.

Toss green tea noodles and grilled vegetables with Mark Ellman's Tomato Miso Vinaigrette dressing.

Lay romaine leaf on plate. Place noodle mixture on top of leaf. Garnish with roasted tomato and opal basil.

Makes 2 portions. *(1 portion = 115 calories, 2.6 grams fat, 14% protein, 66% carbohydrates, 20% fat)*

Cold Somen Salad

Somen is a vermicelli-like Japanese noodle. This is another great way to eat noodles because there is virtually no fat added when you use the right sauce such as the one in this recipe. ❧

1 pkg.	Wheat somen noodles *(10 oz.)*

SAUCE:

1/4 C	Rice vinegar or 2 Tbsp. <u>each</u> rice vinegar and ume plum vinegar
1/4 C	Soy sauce *(low sodium)*
1/2 C	Vegetable broth
1 tsp.	Sesame oil
2 Tbsp.	Mirin
3 Tbsp.	Honey, barley malt, or brown rice syrup

VEGETABLES:

1	Carrot, thinly sliced
1/2	Japanese cucumber, julienned
2 C	Leafy lettuce or won bok, shredded
1/2 pkg.	Radish sprouts or bean sprouts
6-8 large	Shiitake mushrooms *(fresh)*, stems removed
3	Green onion, cut thin diagonally *(garnish)*
1/3 C	Chinese parsley, coarsely chopped *(garnish)*

MARINADE FOR SHIITAKE:

1 Tbsp.	Sesame seeds, toasted and crushed
1/2 tsp.	Sesame oil
1 Tbsp.	Soy sauce or tamari *(low sodium)*
1 Tbsp.	Rice vinegar
1 tsp.	Honey

Cook noodles according to package directions; rinse and drain well. Arrange 8 small mounds of noodles on a large platter; cover and chill.

In a saucepan, combine all sauce ingredients and bring to a boil; lower heat and simmer for 2 minutes. Chill.

Bring a medium saucepan of water to a boil, and have a bowl of ice water ready to cool the vegetables. Blanch the bean sprouts for 10 seconds, remove and place in ice water, and transfer to a small bowl when cool. Repeat this process with the shiitakes, blanching them for 20 seconds.

Combine the marinade ingredients for shiitakes in a small bowl. Slice the shiitakes into slivers, and toss with marinade.

To serve, arrange the prepared vegetables over the chilled noodles. Garnish with green onion and Chinese parsley. Serve with cold sauce.

Makes 4 portions. *(1 portion = 410 calories, 3.7 grams fat, 14% protein, 76% carbohydrates, 8% fat)*

Manauwea (Ogo) Salad

This is a seaweed salad, a cross between Hawaiian and Japanese, that is a great way to get calcium. ❧

1 lb.	Manauwea or ogo seaweed
1 large	Tomato, cut into thin wedges
1/2 large	Round onion, julienne sliced
3 Tbsp.	Vinegar
3 Tbsp.	Sugar
1 tsp.	Ginger, finely grated

Rinse and clean seaweed. Place into a large colander and blanch with hot water *(will turn color)*. Rinse immediately with cold water and chop into 2" pieces. Place into a large bowl with tomatos and onions.

Mix vinegar, sugar, and ginger. Pour over vegetables, toss.

Portion into 4-ounce servings *(about 1/2 cup)* and refrigerate at least 1 hour.

Makes 6 *(1/2-cup)* portions. *(1 portion = 11 calories, 0.1 gram fat, 16% protein, 76% carbohydrates, 7% fat)*

Mountain Fern (Ho'i'o) Salad

This is made of the tender fern shoots that are used in traditional diets of many cultures and is a food that is native to Hawaii. ∽

5 bunches	Fern *(ho'i'o)* , cleaned, cut into 1" pieces
5 large	Tomatoes, cut into quarters
2 large	Maui onions, julienne cut
1/4 C	Sugar
1/4 C	Vinegar
1 finger	Ginger, finely grated

Toss together fern, onion, and tomatoes.

In separate bowl, mix vinegar, sugar and ginger. Pour over vegetables.

Portion into 10, 1-cup servings and refrigerate at least 1 hour.

Makes 10 portions. *(1 portion = 56 calories, 0.6 grams fat, 27% protein, 65% carbohydrates, 8% fat)*

Watercress or Sweet Potato Leaf Salad

This is an excellent salad for calcium as are most dark leafy greens. A mere ounce of watercress contains 43 mg of calcium and 1,400 IU of vitamin A (as beta carotene). ❧

2 bunches	Watercress or sweet potato leaf
5 medium	Tomatoes, diced
3 medium	Round onions, diced
2 large	Lemons

Soak watercress or sweet potato leaf in water for 1 hour.

Rinse and cut in 1/4" pieces.

Mix watercress or sweet potato leaf with tomatoes and onions in a large bowl. Squeeze in lemons.

Chill before serving.

Makes 8 portions. *(1 portion = 43 calories, 0.4 gram fat, 18% protein, 75% carbohydrates, 7% fat)*

Watercress & Bean Sprout Namul

This is a traditional Korean dish that is a tasty vegetable side dish high in calcium and low in fat. ❦

1 bunch	Watercress
1 pkg.	Bean sprouts *(12 oz.)*
2 Tbsp.	Soy sauce
2 Tbsp.	Vinegar
2 Tbsp.	Sesame seed, toasted
2 Tbsp.	Green onion, chopped
1/4 tsp.	Red pepper, ground
1/8 tsp.	Garlic, minced
1/2 tsp.	Sugar

Rinse watercress to clean and remove and discard tough stems. Cut watercress into 1-1/2" lengths. Blanch the watercress and bean sprouts, then drain well.

In a bowl, combine remaining ingredients; add blanched vegetables and mix well. Chill.

Makes 6 portions. *(1 portion = 44 calories, 1.6 grams fat, 26% protein, 45% carbohydrates, 29% fat)*

Great Caesar Salad

The traditional Caesar Salad can be a fine meal in itself, and is often mixed and tossed at tableside in American, French, and Italian restaurants with great panache. You can serve this to guests, with a flourish, or keep the secret to yourself. But whatever you do, rest assured that this version eliminates the anchovies and raw egg — two possibly problematic ingredients in the traditional version of this dish. Most of the fatty olive oil is also eliminated from the dressing. In the process, the taste is actually improved! So enjoy this traditional treat, especially on those evenings when you're too tired to cook but know you deserve something special. ∾

SALAD INGREDIENTS:

1 head	Endive, trimmed
1 head	Red leaf lettuce, torn into pieces
1/4 C	**Arugula** *(also called Rocket)*, **torn to pieces**
1/4 C	**Radicchio** *(a small-leaf Mediterranean lettuce)*
1/2 C	**Oil-free croutons** *(low-fat, store-bought)*
	Black pepper, ground, to taste

There are many excellent low-fat Caesar Salad dressings on the shelves of your health food store. Or, if you have time and want something special, make your own, as follows. If you like the addition of a splash of sherry but don't have time to make your own dressing, just add a tablespoonful to your bottled salad dressing and mix well before using. A very nice touch!

GREAT CAESAR SALAD DRESSING:

2 Tbsp.	Roasted garlic
1/4 C	Sherry cooking wine
1 tsp.	Lemon juice *(fresh)*
1 tsp.	Salt, to taste
1 tsp.	Extra virgin olive oil
1/4 tsp.	Rosemary *(fresh)*, minced
1 Tbsp.	Dijon mustard
1 tsp.	A.1.® Steak Sauce
Dash	Tabasco®, to taste

Toss greens, then dress with store-bought dressing. Or, if making your own dressing *(above)*, pre-mix salad dressing by whisking ingredients together in a bowl. Set aside.

Mix and toss salad, chill, add dressing and dust with pepper just before serving. *Excellent with a side of garlic bread.*

Makes 2 portions as an entrée and 4 portions as side dish. *(1 entrée portion = 154 calories, 3.2 grams fat, 16% protein, 61% carbohydrates, 23% fat) (1 side dish portion = 77 calories, 1.6 grams fat, 16% protein, 61% carbohydrates, 23% fat)*

Miso Potato Salad

This dish combines Japanese and American cuisine into a blend that perfectly illustrates what is unique and delicious about Island food. This dish saves well when refrigerated. You can make it at home and take to the office to really dress up your lunch.

This potato salad is full of flavor but without the high-fat content of mayonnaise. A tablespoon of mayonnaise contains 99 calories and 11 grams of fat while a tablespoon of miso is 35 calories and only 1 gram of fat. This is a fast and healthy alternative to other potato salads. ∾

1 large	Russet potato
2 Tbsp.	Red miso paste
1 Tbsp.	Sweet pickle juice
2 Tbsp.	Sweet pickles, minced fine
1/4 tsp.	Mustard *(prepared, not dry)*

Microwave whole, scrubbed potato on high, for about 4 minutes, or until easy to pierce with a fork.

Remove, cool in freezer for 1 minute. In the meantime mix all other ingredients in a bowl.

Remove potato from freezer and chop into 1/2" cubes. Mix with other ingredients, mashing slightly if you wish to provide variety in texture.

Makes 1 portion. *(1 portion = 257 calories, 2.3 grams fat, 11% protein, 81% carbohydrates, 8% fat)*

Peter Merriman's Mixed Green Vegetable Salad with Ka`u Gold® Potatoes

3-4 oz.	Summer greens
1 lb.	Ka`u Gold® or Yukon Gold® potatoes or other white potatoes
1	Maui onion, sliced
1/2 lb.	Broccoli, minced fine
1	Pineapple *(fresh)*, cut into chunks
	Dijon Vinaigrette *(use as much as you need)*

Wash and boil potatoes until tender. Soak in cold water. Peel and cut into cubes.

Wash summer greens and drain thoroughly. Lay in a salad bowl.

Mix cubed potatoes, onion, broccoli, pineapple and Dijon Vinaigrette. Place on summer greens and serve immediately.

DIJON VINAIGRETTE DRESSING:

1 box	Mori Nu Tofu®
1/3 C	Grey Poupon® Dijon mustard
1/3 C	Red wine vinegar
1/4 tsp.	Black pepper, ground

Place all ingredients in a food processor and blend until smooth. Place in a covered container and store in refrigerator for up to 1 week. Makes 8 portions. *(1 portion = 130 calories, 1.6 grams fat, 13% protein, 76% carbohydrates, 11% fat)*

Carrot-Celery-Pepper Sticks & Garden Dip

Using dips with vegetables makes eating raw or cooked vegetables more fun. This dip is a good example. Another great dip is the hummus found in my original **Dr. Shintani's Eat More, Weigh Less® Diet** *book on page 235.*
ભ

VEGETABLES:

4 large	Carrots
1	Green bell pepper
4 sticks	Celery
	Other vegetables of choice

Peel carrots, cut into more or less uniform strips. Cut celery similarly. Core pepper, cut into similar-sized strips. Plate on crudité tray, or plate. In the center, put a bowl of Garden Dip. You may also serve flowerettes of broccoli and cauliflower.

GARDEN DIP:

1 C	Green peas *(frozen and thawed, or canned),* drained
1/4 C	Avocado
1/4 C	Green onion, chopped fine
	Salt and pepper, to taste
1/8 C	Water
1 clove	Garlic, minced

Blend all ingredients until creamy. Garnish with pimientos, for color.

Makes 8 portions. *(1 portion = 49 calories, 1.1 grams fat, 14% protein, 66% carbohydrates, 19% fat)*

Lomi Tomato

This is a vegetarian version of "Lomi Salmon" which is a standard modern Hawaiian lu'au food. People are surprised how good this is, but they shouldn't be. Why? Because these days there is often not much salmon in the Lomi Salmon anyway and people still like it. So, why not try it without the salmon and thus eliminate the cholesterol. ଓ

5	Tomatoes, diced
8	Green onions, thinly sliced
1 medium	Onion, finely chopped
1-2 Tbsp.	Cider vinegar
1 tsp.	Hawaiian salt
3-5 drops	Tabasco® sauce

Combine all ingredients and chill thoroughly.

Makes 8 portions. *(1 portion = 23 calories, 0.2 gram fat, 15% protein, 78% carbohydrates, 7% fat)*

Fragrant Salad

This is a variation on a Japanese favorite – vinegared vegetables ("namasu"). Just mix together, then dress to taste with salt and mirin, a widely available form of alcohol-free, thick sake. ०२

5 medium	Radishes, scrubbed and grated fine
1 large	Cucumber, scrubbed and sliced to 1" coins
1/4 C	Cabbage, grated
2 Tbsp.	Lemon peel, grated
3 Tbsp.	Lemon juice
1/2 tsp.	Salt, or to taste
1/2 Tbsp.	Maple syrup
	Mirin, to taste

Mix lemon juice and maple syrup in a small bowl. Set aside.

In a serving bowl, toss together vegetables and lemon peel. Dress with lemon juice and maple syrup mixture, add salt and mirin.

Makes 4 portions. *(1 portion = 24 calories, 0.2 gram fat, 9% protein, 87% carbohydrates, 5% fat)*

Summer Relish Salad

1	Red bell pepper, diced coarsely
1 small	Zucchini squash, chopped
1 C	Corn *(fresh)*, steamed lightly then scraped from cob
1 C	Red onion, chopped
2 Tbsp.	Mint *(fresh)*, chopped
1/8 tsp.	Salt
2 Tbsp.	Balsamic vinegar

Combine all ingredients in a small bowl, then serve.

Makes 2 generous portions. *(1 portion = 116 calories, 0.5 gram fat, 14% protein, 83% carbohydrates, 4% fat)*

Green Bean Salad

1 C	Green beans *(canned or cooked)*, drained
1/2 head	Lettuce, broken into bite-sized pieces
1 C	Tomatoes, chopped
1 C	Onions, diced
	Salad dressing of choice *(low fat)*

Toss all ingredients together, then dress and serve.

Makes 4 portions. *(1 portion = 49 calories, 1.1 grams fat, 15% protein, 66% carbohydrates, 19% fat)*

Asparagus Artichoke Salad

1/2 C	Marinated artichoke hearts *(bottled)*, rinse off oil
1 pkg.	Asparagus, 8-oz. frozen and thawed, drained well
1/2 C	Red onion, chopped
1 C	Red bib lettuce, torn into bite-sized shreds
1 sm. can	Pickled beet slices, drained, juice reserved
1/2 C	Beet juice from pickled beets
2 Tbsp.	Balsamic vinegar
1 tsp.	A.1.® Steak Sauce
	Salt, to taste
	Black pepper, freshly ground, to taste

Mix last three ingredients into a dressing, toss all other ingredients together, then dress and serve. Makes 4 portions.

Green Papaya Salad

1 clove	Garlic
2	Hawaiian chili peppers
1/2 lb.	Green papaya, peeled, seeded, and shredded
1	Tomato, sliced
2 Tbsp.	Thai fish sauce *(optional)*
3 Tbsp.	Lime juice
	Sugar, to taste
1 head	Lettuce or cabbage, shredded

Grind garlic and chili peppers.

Combine shredded papaya, sliced tomato, fish sauce, lime juice and pepper-garlic mixture and mix well.

Serve on a bed of lettuce or cabbage.

A little sugar will sweeten the tartness of this popular Thai salad.

Makes 4-6 portions *(5 cups).* (1 portion = 48 calories, 0.3 grams fat, 16% protein, 78% carbohydrates, 5% fat)

* From **Wai`anae Diet Cookbook** (currently out of print), page 21

Fresh Citrus Salad

This is an excellent breakfast or quick-lunch dish, especially when served with a side of cinnamon toast. ରୁ

2	Kiwi fruit, peeled and sliced
2	Bananas, cut into 1" coins
1/2	Papaya, halved, seeded, peeled, and cubed
2 tsp.	Lime zest
1 Tbsp.	Green onion with stems, finely chopped
1 tsp.	Lime juice *(fresh)*

Mix all fruits together, then mix all other ingredients and whisk, to use for dressing. Add dressing just before serving.

Makes 4 portions as an entrée, 6 portions as a side dish. *(1 entrée portion = 99 calories, 0.5 grams fat, 5% protein, 91% carbohydrates, 4% fat) (1 side dish portion = 66 calories, 0.4 grams fat, 5% protein, 91% carbohydrates, 1% fat)*

Entrées

Lawalu Chicken

This is chicken or fish steamed in the traditional Hawaiian way. This is a great way to prepare food without any added oil. ☙

5 to 7	Taro *(lu'au)* leaves
3 oz.	Chicken or fish, deboned and skinless
2 pinches	Salt
2 medium	Ti leaves

Cut taro stems from taro leaves. Wash taro leaves. Stack 5 to 7 taro leaves on each other. Place chicken in center of taro leaves. Add a pinch of salt *(optional)* and wrap taro leaves to cover the chicken.

Wrap in ti leaves and steam in a covered container for approximately four hours.

Makes 1 portion. *(1 portion for chicken = 194 calories, 3.4 gm. fat, 64% protein, 20% carbohydrates, 15% fat) (1 portion for fish = 138 calories, 1.5 grams fat, 63% protein, 27% carbohydrates, 9% fat)*

Variation:

Wrap sweet potato or taro chunks in the taro leaves with the chicken or fish.

See page 55 for taro cooking instructions and precautions for taro and taro leaves.

Chicken Breast In Phyllo

Chicken Breast In Phyllo was a dish served on the Mediter-anean portion of the "HawaiiDiet™ Study". This dish has a little dairy but is still much lower in fat than dishes of this type because we cut down the oils and fats. Even so, go easy on the feta cheese, as it is a main source of the fat in this recipe. ∂

	Garlic Mist®
1/2 C	Onions, minced
1/2 lb.	Mushrooms, minced
4 Tbsp.	Parsley, minced
2 tsp.	Garlic, minced
1/4 tsp.	Oregano
1 Tbsp.	Whole wheat pastry flour
1/2 C	Dry white wine
	Salt and pepper, to taste
20 oz.	Chicken breasts, boneless, skinless, and cut into 1/2" pieces
	Garlic powder
8 sheets	Phyllo pastry
2 C	Whole wheat bread crumbs
1/4 lb.	Feta cheese, crumbled
1/2 pkg.	Spinach *(frozen)*, chopped

Preheat oven 350° F.

In a skillet, sauté garlic and onions in white wine and set aside.

Sauté mushrooms and 2 tablespoons of parsley in white wine. Season with salt and pepper to taste. Remove from pan and set aside.

In same skillet, spray Garlic Mist® and sauté chicken breasts until lightly browned. Remove from heat.

Place a piece of wax paper on the counter and lay one sheet of phyllo over it. Lightly spray with Garlic Mist®. Sprinkle with bread crumbs mixed with parsley.

Lay a second sheet of phyllo over the bread crumbs. Place chopped chicken breast on lower half of phyllo. Spread a quarter of the mushroom mixture and a layer of spinach over the chicken. Fold up sides of phyllo over chicken "envelope style." Repeat with remaining chicken.

Spray chicken rolls lightly with Garlic Mist® and lay seam side down on an ungreased baking sheet. Bake for 35 minutes or until golden brown. Serve warm.

TOMATO AND HERB SAUCE:

1 tsp.	Olive oil
1/2 C	Maui onion
3 cloves	Garlic, minced
1/2 C	Mushrooms, sliced
1/2 C	Wine
1	Tomato, peeled, seeded, and chopped
1 tsp.	Oregano

Sauté onion and garlic in olive oil. Add mushrooms, tomato, oregano, and wine.

For presentation place the phyllo rolls in the middle of the plate and drizzle sauce around the rolls. Garnish with parsley.

Makes 8 portions. *(1 portion = 360 calories, 8.8 grams fat, 36% protein, 40% carbohydrates, 24% fat)*

Taro Hekka

Hekka is synonymous with sukiyaki. You can do this with any of your favorite vegetables, and you can invent your own dish. ‿

1/2 lb.	Chicken, skinless, boneless, sliced thin
2 C	Taro, cooked, cut up in chunks*
2 C	Bamboo shoots, sliced thin
2 C	Shiitake mushrooms, soaked and sliced
2 Tbsp.	Maple syrup or other sweetener
2 C	Water or vegetable broth for mushrooms
1 bunch	Watercress, chopped
1 can	Water chestnuts, sliced thin
1 bunch	Green onions, sliced thin
4 cloves	Garlic *(medium-size)*, crushed
	Pam® No Stick Cooking Spray
	Soy sauce *(low sodium)*, to taste

Soak shiitake mushrooms in 2 cups of water or vegetable broth, then slice.

Stir fry chicken in a hot wok sprayed with Pam®. Add garlic. Add bamboo shoots, sliced shiitake mushrooms, and sweetener. Add water chestnuts, cooked taro, and watercress.

Stir fry for 5 minutes, cover with lid, and turn off. The heat from the wok will continue the cooking process and vegetables will be crunchy. Add low sodium soy sauce to taste.

Makes 10 *(1 cup)* servings. *(1 portion = 118 calories, 2.2 grams fat, 28% protein, 56% carbohydrates, 16% fat)*

* *See page 55 for taro cooking instructions and precautions for taro and pages 188-189 for taro leaves.*

Chicken Papaya*

3 C	Chicken, skinless, chopped into small pieces
1 small	Onion, diced
2	Carrots, cut into 1/2" pieces
2 small	Green papayas, skin and seeds removed, cut into cubes
2 stalks	Celery, sliced into 1/2" pieces
2 large	Ripe tomatoes, cut into wedges
1-2	Bay leaves
4 cloves	Garlic
pinch	Oregano leaves
	Salt and pepper, to taste

In a saucepan, cover chicken in water and simmer until tender, skimming fat. *(If you have time, refrigerate until fat separates, about 15 minutes.)*

Add remaining ingredients, except tomatoes. Simmer 1 hour. Add tomatoes and salt and pepper to taste. Cover and simmer for 10 minutes.

Makes 6 to 8 *(1 cup)* portions. *(1 portion = 108 calories, 1.8 grams fat, 53% protein, 33% carbohydrates, 14% fat)*

* From **Wai`anae Diet Cookbook** (currently out of print), page 32

*Chicken Broccoli**

1 lb.	Chicken breasts, boneless and skinless, cut in small strips
2	Onions, sliced and quartered
3 cloves	Garlic, crushed
3 slices	Ginger, crushed
1 lb.	Broccoli, chopped
1 small	Carrot, cut into julienne
1/2 tsp.	Black pepper
3 Tbsp.	Soy sauce *(optional)*
2 C	Water

In a pan, combine 1/2 cup water, ginger, garlic, and onions. Cook until tender. Add chicken and stir for 5 minutes or until meat turns white. Add 1-1/2 cups of water, pepper, and soy sauce. Cover pan and let simmer for 10 minutes. Add broccoli and carrots. Stir, cover the pan, and simmer for another 5 minutes.

Makes 6 to 8 *(1 cup)* portions. *(1 portion = 132 calories, 2.4 grams fat, 61% protein, 24% carbohydrates, 16% fat)*

* From **Wai`anae Diet Cookbook** (currently out of print), page 30

Hula Grill's Ginger Pineapple Chicken

This is a creation of Chef Peter Merriman. The sauce can be used in any stir fry or entreé with or without chicken. It was served at the Governor's mansion at the completion of the HawaiiDiet™ Program in January 1997. ❧

1-1/2 tsp.	Garlic, chopped
1-1/2 tsp.	Ginger, minced
4 oz.	Chicken breast, sliced
4 oz.	Carrot, sliced for stir fry
4 oz.	Celery, sliced for stir fry
4 oz.	Onion, chopped for stir fry
1 oz.	Broccoli, cut up for stir fry
1/2 can	Water chestnuts, sliced
2 oz.	Pineapple *(fresh)*, diced

STIR-FRY SAUCE:

2 Tbsp.	Hoisin sauce
2 Tbsp.	Sweet soy sauce *(Kecap Manis)*
2 Tbsp.	Soy sauce
2 Tbsp.	Pineapple sauce or puréed pineapple
1 Tbsp.	Cornstarch

In a small bowl, mix first four stir-fry sauce ingredients, then add cornstarch and mix thoroughly so there are no lumps. Set aside.

Water-sauté garlic, ginger, and onion in wok or skillet until light brown. Add chicken and cook until golden brown, adding water if necessary. Add in carrots, celery, and broccoli and cook until crispy-tender. Add water chestnuts and stir-fry sauce and cook until it thickens. Add pineapple chunks and serve immediately over hot rice.

Makes 4 portions. *(1 portion = 112 calories, 2.4 grams fat, 38% protein, 43% carbohydrates, 19% fat)*

Noodles with Chicken – Filipino Style *(Pansit)*

2 cloves	Garlic, minced
1 slice	Ginger root, minced
2	Celery stalks, sliced thin
1/2 lb.	Chicken breast, skinless, cut in thin 1" x 2" strips
1/4 head	Cabbage, thinly sliced
1/2 C	Chicken broth
1/2 lb.	Noodles *(fine, Bihon rice sticks)*, cooked and drained
1 sm. pkg.	Opai *(small dried shrimp)*
2	Bell peppers, chopped
5 Tbsp.	Patis *(optional)*
3	Carrots, thinly sliced
	Pam® No Stick Cooking Spray *(optional)*

Sauté garlic and ginger in Pam® or 1/4 cup water, until tender. Add chicken with patis. Cook until brown, approximately 15 minutes. Add celery, cabbage, chicken broth, bell pepper, and carrots. Cook until tender, approximately 10 minutes. Add noodles and opai and cook for 30 minutes until noodles soften.

Makes 8 *(1 cup)* portions. *(1 portion = 130 calories, 2 grams fat, 11% fat)*

Peter Merriman's Baked Ono

This is another tasty recipe contributed by one of Hawaii's great regional chefs. The sauce used on this dish is versatile and can be used on vegetables or other entrées as well. ∝

15 oz.	Ono fillets *(enough to yield 12 oz. cooked)*
2 Tbsp.	Lime juice
1/2 tsp.	Garlic, minced
2 tsp.	Shallot, minced
1/2 Tbsp.	Rosemary *(fresh)*, chopped
1/2 Tbsp.	Thyme *(fresh)*, chopped
1/2 C	Shiitake mushrooms *(fresh)*, sliced
1-1/2 tsp.	Ginger *(fresh)*, julienned
Dash	White pepper
1/8 C	Chinese parsley, chopped
1 small	Carrot, julienned
1/3 C	Water
3 Tbsp.	Green onion, chopped

Place ono fillets in baking dish. Combine lime juice, garlic, shallot, herbs, mushroom, ginger, pepper, Chinese parsley, and carrot; pour over fillets. Add water and cover with foil.

Bake in a 350° F. oven for 15 to 20 minutes. Garnish with chopped green onion.

Makes 4 *(2-ounce)* portions. *(1 portion = 101 calories, 1.5 grams fat, 53% protein, 30% carbohydrates, 17 % fat)*

Roy's Broiled Hawaiian Swordfish in Miso

Chef Roy Yamaguchi shares some of his secrets here. This recipe will be fancy enough for any dinner guest while keeping the fat content at a reasonable level. ❧

MARINADE:

1/3 C	White miso *(shiro miso)*
1-1/2 Tbsp.	Sake
2 tsp.	Brown sugar
2/3 C	Hoisin sauce
1-1/2 Tbsp.	Ginger, minced
1-1/2 Tbsp.	Garlic, minced
1-1/2 Tbsp.	Orange juice *(fresh)*
1 Tbsp.	Chili paste with garlic *(preferably Lan Chi brand)*
4	Swordfish steaks *(about 6 oz. each)*
1 C	Red pickled ginger
1 lb.	Japanese cucumber, seeded, chopped, and peel left on

GARNISH:

2 oz.	Japanese spice sprouts or radish sprouts
1 tsp.	Black sesame seeds
1 tsp.	White sesame seeds, toasted
	Guacamole *(optional)*

In a large bowl, mix all the marinade ingredients. Add swordfish pieces to marinade and let sit in the refrigerator for 4 hours.

Preheat the grill. Purée the red pickled ginger in a food processor until smooth. Drain in a sieve. Likewise, purée the cucumbers in a food processor and drain in sieve. Set red pickled ginger and cucumbers aside.

Grill swordfish pieces for 45 seconds to 60 seconds on each side *(for medium rare)*. On each serving plate, lay out a circle of puréed cucumber and a smaller concentric circle of pickled ginger. Place the swordfish steak on the puréed ginger. Garnish with a toss with the sprouts and sesame seeds. Serve with a little guacamole, if desired.

The marinade "cooks" the fish to a certain degree, so keep the grilling time to a bare minimum so the fish will not dry out.

Makes 8 *(3-ounce)* portions. *(1 portion with guacamole = 217 calories, 6.0 grams fat, 45% protein, 30% carbohydrates, 25% fat)*

Roy's Blackened 'Ahi with Soy-Mustard Sauce

Hawaii is proud of Chef Roy Yamaguchi. This is one of his signature dishes, a Pacific version of a Cajun classic. I have modified it slightly to reduce fat content. Roy adds that the sandalwood in the blackening spice is optional but gives a reddish color and an intriguing flavor. (You can use Yogi brand by calling them in New Orleans at 504-486-5538). Or, if you prefer, you can use 1/4 cup of any Cajun spice blend instead of making your own blackening spice.

Soy-Mustard Sauce:

1/4 C	Coleman's mustard powder
2 Tbsp.	Hot water
2 Tbsp.	Rice vinegar, unseasoned
1/4 C	Soy sauce

Blackening Spice:

1-1/2 Tbsp.	Paprika
1/2 Tbsp.	Cayenne pepper
1/2 Tbsp.	Pure red chili powder
1/4 tsp.	White pepper, freshly ground
1/2 Tbsp.	Sandalwood *(ground, optional)*

1	'Ahi tuna fillet about 2" thick and 5" long *(about 8 oz.)*

Garnish:

2 or 3 Tbsp.	Red pickled ginger
1/2 tsp.	Black sesame seeds

1 oz.	Japanese spice sprouts or sunflower sprouts *(top 2 inches only)*
1 Tbsp.	Yellow bell peppers, seeded and diced *(optional)*
1 Tbsp.	Cucumber, cut into matchsticks *(optional)*

Mix the hot water and mustard powder into a paste. Let the mixture sit for a few minutes to develop the flavor. Mix in the vinegar and soy sauce, then strain through a fine sieve, and chill in the refrigerator.

Mix paprika, cayenne pepper, chili powder, white pepper, and sandalwood *(optional)* on a plate, and dredge 'ahi on both sides. Heat a cast-iron skillet that is lightly oiled, and sear 'ahi on high heat for 15 seconds per side *(for rare)* to 60 seconds per side *(for medium-rare)*. Cut into 16 thin strips.

On each serving plate, lay out 4 strips of fish in a pinwheel or cross shape. Put a little Soy-Mustard Sauce in the spaces between the fish.

To garnish, put a small mound of red pickled ginger on two of the Soy-Mustard Sauce pinwheel quadrants, and sprinkle the sesame seeds over the other two quadrants. Arrange the spice sprouts, bell pepper, and cucumber at the very center of this pinwheel.

Makes 4 *(2-ounce)* portions. *(1 portion = 139 calories, 4.3 grams fat, 49% protein, 25% carbohydrates, 26% fat)*

Salmon Hot Pot

Salmon Hot Pot was a favorite on the HawaiiDiet™ Study and was carried over to the Hawaii Health Program. ଔ

6 C	Water
1/2	Maui onion
5 cloves	Garlic
4 Tbsp.	Ginger, crushed
1/2 C	Sake
1-1/2 Tbsp.	Mirin
1 Tbsp.	Soy sauce
3/4 Tbsp.	Hawaiian salt
2 large	Potatoes, diced
3	Carrots, sliced diagonally
5 oz.	Salmon fillets, cut into 1" chunks
8 oz.	Tofu *(firm)*
4 stalks	Green onion
1-1/2 C	Won bok cabbage, sliced thinly
7 oz.	Mushrooms *(fresh)*, sliced
	Chinese parsley

Water-sauté onion, garlic, and ginger. Add sake, mirin, soy sauce, and salt and water. Bring mixture to a boil for 10 minutes. Add carrots and potatoes, and cook until tender. Add salmon and cook until almost done. Toss in tofu, won bok, mushrooms, and green onion. Garnish with Chinese parsley and serve.

Makes 4 portions. *(1 portion = 250 calories, 5.6 grams fat, 31% protein, 48% carbohydrates, 21% fat)*

Squid or Fish Lu'au

This is another traditional Hawaiian dish that is prepared without oil. ca

4 C	Taro *(lu'au)* leaves, precooked
3 oz.	Squid *(octopus)* or fish, cut into bite-sized pieces
	Salt, to taste
1-1/2 C	Water

Taro (lu'au) leaves come precooked in the frozen section. Should you want to make your own, see pages 188-189 for cooking instructions and precautions.

Put the precooked taro *(lu'au)* leaves and water in a medium-size cooking pot. Bring to a boil, then lower temperature to medium. Add squid *(octopus)* or fish and simmer 30 minutes or until the squid is tender. Stir occasionally. Add salt to taste.

Makes 3 portions *(1 ounce squid or fish plus 1-1/3 cups of taro leaves).* (1 portion = 171 calories, 2.2 grams fat, 39% protein, 50% carbohydrates, 10% fat)

Shrimp with Snowpeas & Mushrooms

This was a dish used in the HawaiiDiet™ Study to represent a traditional Asian-style meal where a small amount of flesh was used with a large amount of vegetables. ભ

MARINADE:

1 Tbsp.   Soy sauce
1 Tbsp.   Rice vinegar
1/4 tsp. 5-spice powder *(cloves, fennel, cinnamon, anise and ginger)*
6 oz.   Shrimp, peeled and deveined

SEASONING:

1 Tbsp.   Garlic, minced
1 Tbsp.   Ginger, minced

VEGETABLES:

6 oz.   Snowpeas *(about 2 cups)*, stems and strings removed
6 oz.   Mushrooms

SAUCE:

3/4 C   Vegetable broth
1/4 C   Dry white wine
1 Tbsp.   Soy sauce
1 Tbsp.   Cornstarch, dissolved in 2 Tbsp. cold water
          Canola oil spray

Combine soy sauce, rice vinegar, and 5-spice powder in bowl. Put shrimp in soy sauce mixture and marinate 20 to 30 minutes.

Combine seasonings in a small bowl.

Combine snowpeas and water chestnuts in a bowl.

Combine sauce ingredients in a bowl.

Heat a nonstick wok over high heat for 2 minutes. Spray wok with canola spray *(carefully, avoiding flame if using gas stove)* and add seasonings and stir fry 15 seconds. Add snowpeas and mushrooms. Cook for 2 minutes. Add shrimp and marinade. Stir until it boils. Add cornstarch and stir 1 minute until thick. Serve.

Makes 3 portions. *(1 portion = 181 calories, 1.7 grams fat, 46% protein, 44% carbohydrates, 10% fat)*

Shrimp with Green Papaya

This variation on a traditional Thai dish was used on the study and the Hawaii Health Program. ∞

3-4 oz.	Shrimp *(to yield 3 ounces cooked)*, may use 2 oz. tiny dried shrimp
1 small	Onion, diced
2	Carrots, cut into 1/2" pieces
2 small	Green papayas, skin and seeds removed, cut into cubes
2 stalks	Celery, sliced into 1/2" pieces
2 large	Tomatoes *(ripe)*, cut into wedges
2	Bay leaves
4 cloves	Garlic, minced
pinch	Oregano leaves
	Salt, to taste
	Pepper, to taste

Simmer shrimp in a small amount of water until pink. Add remaining ingredients, except tomatoes. Simmer 1 hour. Add tomatoes and salt and pepper to taste. Cover and simmer for 10 minutes.

Makes 3 portions. *(1 portion = 129 calories, 0.9 gram fat, 25% protein, 69% carbohydrates, 6% fat)*

Chop Chae

This is a "long rice" or "cellophane noodle" dish made Korean style that uses seasonings to give it a golden, amber-brown appearance. ❧

1 bundle	Long rice
1/2 bunch	Watercress, cut into 2" lengths
1/2 pkg.	Bean sprouts
1 small	Onion, sliced
1 medium	Carrot, julienned
1 Tbsp.	Garlic, minced
1/2 tsp.	Ginger *(fresh)*, grated
	Canola oil cooking spray
1/2 C	Vegetable broth

SAUCE:

3 Tbsp.	Soy sauce
1 Tbsp.	Ko choo jung
2 tsp.	Honey
1 tsp.	Sea salt
1/4 tsp.	Pepper

Soak long rice in cold water for 15 minutes. Drain and cut into 2" lengths. Drop into 1 quart boiling water, turn heat off, and let stand for 5 minutes. Drain.

Spray nonstick skillet with oil. Sauté onions, carrots, garlic, and ginger until onions are just limp. Add watercress; cook until crisp-tender. Add sauce ingredients, then bean sprouts and vegetable broth. Stir in long rice, and serve immediately. Makes 6 portions. *(1 portion = 145 calories, 0.5 gram fat, 12% protein, 84% carbohydrates, 3% fat)*

Pho

Vietnamese food is the rage in Honolulu's Chinatown. Pho (pronouced "fa") is a traditional Vietnamese noodle soup that was served on the HawaiiDiet™ Study and Hawaii Health Programs, sometimes for breakfast. ❧

3 quarts	Chicken-flavored broth *(made with chicken-flavored bouillon cubes and water)*
1-1/2 Tbsp.	Salt
1 piece	Ginger, 2-1/2"
1	Yellow onion
2 whole	Star anise
4 whole	Cloves
1/2 stick	Cinnamon
1 stick	Sugar cane, sliced into 4 lengthwise strips
1/8 C	Fish sauce
1/2 lb.	Rice sticks *(dried)*, small

CONDIMENTS:

2	Green onion stalks, chopped
1/4 bunch	Chinese parsley, chopped
1/2 lb.	Bean sprouts
12 sprigs	Thai basil sprigs *(fresh)*
1	Lime, cut into wedges
	Chili pepper paste with garlic

Soak rice sticks in hot water, then drain.

Dry roast ginger and onions by placing them in a skillet over high heat. Cook 20 minutes on each side evenly without charring skins.

Place chicken-flavored broth into large stock pot. Add salt, ginger, onions, star anise, cloves, cinnamon stick, sugar cane, and fish sauce. Simmer about 2 hours.

Arrange the condiments on a platter and set aside.

Place drained rice sticks in separate bowls and pour broth over noodles. Garnish with condiments of choice. Serve piping hot.

Makes 4 portions. *(1 portion = 244 calories, 0.5 grams fat, 6% protein, 92% carbohydrates, 2% fat)*

Chickenless Long Rice

This is a variation on the traditional lu'au-style chicken long rice. It can be done with or without chicken. Both can be low-fat selections if prepared properly. Everyone should try this at least once to see that it can be tasty either way. ❧

1/2 tsp.	Sesame oil
1 large	Round onion, diced
3 cloves	Garlic, crushed
2 quarts	Water
3 Tbsp.	Chicken-flavored vegetarian broth *(instant)*
1" piece	Ginger root, peeled and crushed
8 oz.	Long rice
1/2 C	Shiitake mushrooms *(dried)*, soaked, sliced
1/2 C	Green onions

Soak shiitake mushrooms in water to cover for 10 to 15 minutes. Drain, slice, and set aside.

Soak long rice in water to cover for 10 to 15 minutes.

Sauté onion and garlic in sesame oil until onions are slightly browned. Add water, instant broth mix, and ginger; simmer together at least 10 minutes. Drain long rice and cut into 3" lengths. Add to broth and cook until noodles are done. Add shiitake mushrooms and stir. Garnish with green onions and serve.

Makes 6 portions. (1 portion = 173 calories, 0.5 gram fat, 7% protein, 90% carbohydrates, 3% fat)

Mu Shu Vegetables*

This is a delicious dish that you can get in Szechwan Chinese restaurants by ordering "mu shu pork" but without the pork and eggs.

Mu shu is actually a Chinese delicacy which is a crinkly dark brown fungus. This is difficult to find but not necessary to this dish.

Hoisin sauce, found in the oriental section of the supermarket or in Chinatown, is a savory plum sauce which can make simple vegetables into a feast. It is on the salty and sweet side, so use carefully. ଓ

1 pkg.	Mung bean sprouts
1/4 head	Won bok or head cabbage, sliced
1/2	Onion, vertically sliced
4	Shiitake mushrooms, soaked and sliced
1/2	Carrot, julienne
1 clove	Garlic *(fresh)*, minced
dash	Sesame oil
	Water and soy sauce, to taste
6 tsp.	Hoisin sauce, to taste
6 pieces	Chinese mu shu fungus *(optional)*
1 bundle	Cellophane noodles, *(optional)*
1/4 head	Cabbage, shredded *(optional)*
12	Whole wheat chapatis or medium-sized tortillas

Slice cabbage and vertically slice onion into thin crescents. Chop mushrooms and cut carrot into matchsticks or grate it into thin strips.

Soak cellophane noodles in water to cover until soft.

In a large skillet or wok, sauté onions in water and a dash of sesame oil until slightly translucent. Then sauté the rest of the vegetables in water and soy sauce.

Spread 1/2 teaspoon of hoisin sauce on the chapati or tortilla. Lay the sautéed vegetables down the middle. If adding, lay softened cellophane noodles and cabbage on top of vegetables. Roll the vegetables *(and noodles)* in the chapati or tortilla.

Makes 12 portions. *(1 portion = 145 calories, 2.0 grams fat, 8% protein, 80% carbohydrates, 12% fat)*

* From **Dr. Shintani's Eat More, Weigh Less® Diet** book, page 148

*Kabobs**

Kabobs can be a festive treat and relatively easy to prepare. They are also another way to use high SMI foods. I got interested in kabobs when a patient of mine said that she had to go to a potluck dinner where they were all making kabobs and didn't know what to bring. I told her she could easily bring delicious vegetable kabobs. The secret, I told her, was in the marinade. The happy ending was that everyone liked her kabobs best, and many of them left the meat off their kabobs and borrowed her marinade. ✑

1 small	Cauliflower, cut into flowerettes
10	String beans or 1 bunch of broccoli, cut into flowerettes
2	Carrots, cut into 1" pieces
3 stalks	Celery, cut into 1" pieces
1/2 block	Tofu *(firm)* or tempeh, cut into cubes *(Tempeh is a soybean product that is fermented just enough to reduce some of the beany taste and gas.)*
	Sea salt, to taste

Bring 2" to 3" of water to a boil and steam tofu or tempeh and vegetables until just tender.

On a skewer, place pieces of carrot, celery, string bean or broccoli, and cauliflower. Place the cauliflower on the end so it will look like a flower on the end of the skewer. Top kabobs with sauce.

Variation:

You can marinate the kabobs in the sauce and then cook over a grill.

Makes 4 portions. *(1 portion = 160 calories, 4.6 grams fat, 30% protein, 46% carbohydrates, 24% fat)*

Sauces for Kabobs

Dijon Marinade

2 Tbsp.	Dijon mustard *(for variation, use other mustards)*
3 Tbsp.	Soy sauce or tamari *(low sodium)*
3 Tbsp.	Lemon juice
2 cloves	Garlic, crushed

Mix ingredients together and use as marinade.

Makes 4 portions. *(1 portion = 15 calories, 0.1 gram fat, 33% protein, 64% carbohydrates, 3% fat)*

Teriyaki Marinade

1/3 C	Soy sauce or tamari *(low sodium)*
2 Tbsp.	Blackstrap molasses or honey
1 Tbsp.	Ginger *(fresh)*, grated
1 clove	Garlic, crushed
2 tsp.	Arrowroot or cornstarch, mixed in 2 tsp. water to dissolve
1 Tbsp.	Sake or white wine *(optional)*
1 Tbsp.	Lemon juice *(optional)*
2 Tbsp.	Water

Combine dissolved arrowroot or cornstarch with other ingredients in a saucepan. Bring to a boil and let cool.

Makes 4 portions. *(1 portion = 47 calories, 0.0 gram fat, 20% protein, 80% carbohydrates, 0% fat)*

Korean Barbecue Sauce

1/3 C	Soy sauce or tamari *(low sodium)*
2 Tbsp.	Blackstrap molasses or honey
3 cloves	Garlic, crushed
2 tsp.	Arrowroot or cornstarch, mixed in 2 tsp. water to dissolve
1/2 tsp.	Sesame oil
1 Tbsp.	Sake or white wine *(optional)*
1 Tbsp.	Lemon juice *(optional)*
2 Tbsp.	Water

Combine dissolved arrowroot or cornstarch with other ingredients in a saucepan. Bring to a boil and let cool.

Makes 4 portions. *(1 portion = 51 calories, 0.6 gram fat, 17% protein, 72% carbohydrates, 11% fat)*

White Wine Marinade

1/2 C	White wine
2 Tbsp.	Lemon juice
2 - 3	Bay leaves

3/4 tsp.   Thyme
         Pepper, to taste

Mix ingredients together and it's ready.

Barbecue Marinade

3/4 C	Ketchup
1/4 C	Lemon juice
3 Tbsp.	Molasses or honey
1/4 C	Steak sauce *(such as A.1.® Steak Sauce)*
1/2 tsp.	Sea salt
	Pepper, to taste

Mix ingredients together in a saucepan. Boil, cover, and simmer for 4 to 5 minutes. Use as marinade.

* *From **Dr. Shintani's Eat More, Weigh Less® Diet** book, pages 194-196*

Hawaiian Savory Stew*

This dish was so well liked despite the fact that it had no meat in it that it was published in the newspapers. You'll be pleasantly surprised at its authentic local flavor. ᙄ

3 Tbsp.	Water
1 large	Onion, chopped
2 cloves	Garlic, minced
1 piece	Ginger *(1")*, mashed
1 box	Seitan *(wheat gluten)*, cut in 1" pieces or 1 C mushrooms
1 Tbsp.	Soy sauce
2 large	Carrots, cut in 1" chunks
2 stalks	Celery, cut in 1" chunks
3	Red potatoes, quartered
1 can	Tomatoes, whole packed
3	Bay leaves
2 C	Vegetable broth
	Water, to cover
	Salt, to taste
	Pepper, to taste
2 Tbsp.	Whole wheat flour dissolved in 4 Tbsp. water
	Tabasco® sauce *(optional)*

Sauté onion and garlic in 3 tablespoons of water in a large pot. Add seitan or mushrooms, ginger, soy sauce, carrots, celery, potatoes, tomatoes, vegetable broth, water to cover, salt, pepper, and bay leaves. Cook until vegetables are tender. Thicken with whole wheat flour dissolved in 4 tablespoons of water.

Serve hot. Zing it with a few drops of Tabasco® sauce.

Makes 6 to 8 portions. *(1 portion (with seitan) = 256 calories, 1.2 grams fat, 32% protein, 64% carbohydrates, 4% fat) (1 portion (with mushrooms) = 132 calories, 0.5 gram fat, 17% protein, 80% carbohydrates, 3% fat)*

* *From **Dr. Shintani's Eat More, Weigh Less**® **Cookbook**, page 205*

Vegetable Stew

This is a variation on a meatless stew that has a nice Mediterranean flavor to it. ख

1 tsp.	Extra virgin olive oil
1 large	Red onion, halved and sliced
2 cloves	Garlic, chopped
1 large	Red bell pepper
1-2/3 C	Tomatoes with juice, crushed, canned
1 large	Carrot, cut into 1" pieces
1 small	Eggplant
3/4 C	Water
2	Potatoes, cut into 1" pieces
2	Zucchini, thickly sliced
4 oz.	Peas
4 oz.	Garbanzo beans
1 C	Green beans, cut
1 tsp.	Salt
1 tsp.	Pepper

In a large saucepan brown the garlic and onion in hot oil. Add red bell pepper and cook for 2 minutes. Add tomatoes and cook for 2 more minutes. Add carrots, eggplant, and water and cook for 2 more minutes. Add potatoes, zucchini, peas, beans, green beans, salt, and pepper and cook for 20 minutes or until potatoes are cooked. Serve hot or cold.

Makes 6 portions. *(1 portion = 175 calories, 2.1 grams fat, 19% protein, 71% carbohydrates, 10% fat)*

Red Chili Lentil Stew

Chef Roy Yamaguchi contributed this spicy, versatile recipe. It can be served as a hot, hearty soup; as a side dish or as a condiment for broiled fish it takes on quite a different flavor. I have modified it slightly to reduce the fat content.
ભ

1 C	Red or brown lentils
1 Tbsp.	Olive oil
1	Onion, finely diced
1-1/2 Tbsp.	Garlic, minced
2 Tbsp.	Carrot, finely diced
2 Tbsp.	Celery, finely diced
3	Bay leaves
1 tsp.	Red chili flakes *(dried)*, crushed
1 lb.	Tomatoes, peeled, seeded, and diced
2 C	Vegetarian chicken broth
1-1/2 C	Tomato juice *(canned)*
2 tsp.	Basil *(fresh)*, julienned
1 tsp.	Thyme *(fresh)*, minced
1 tsp.	Tarragon *(fresh)*, minced
1 Tbsp.	Salt
1/2 tsp.	Sugar
1/2 tsp.	Pepper, freshly ground

VINAIGRETTE:

1/2 Tbsp.	Sherry Vinegar
1 tsp.	Olive oil

In a colander wash lentils under a cold tap. Then soak in a bowl of water for half an hour, drain, and set aside.

Heat the olive oil in a large stockpot, and sauté the onion, garlic, carrot, and celery over high heat about 1 to 2 minutes or until mix is lightly browned. Now stir in the rest of the ingredients except the lentils, sherry vinegar, and remaining olive oil. Continue to stir for about a minute, and then add the lentils. Cook over medium heat for about 30 minutes, or until the lentils are just tender, but before they get mushy.

Whisk together the vinaigrette ingredients just before serving, and stir it into the lentil stew.

Variation:

To prepare this stew as a side dish or a condiment, cut the ingredient quantities in half and omit the vinaigrette. Cook as above, then strain the lentils and reserve the liquid. Spread the lentils on a baking sheet, then refrigerate. Serve cold, or you may warm the lentils in a saucepan along with a little of the reserved liquid.

Makes 6 portions. *(1 portion as entrée = 127 calories, 3.4 grams fat, 20% protein, 57% carbohydrates, 22% fat) (1 portion as side dish = 60 calories, 1.3 grams fat, 21% protein, 60% carbohydrates, 18% fat)*

Vegetable Laulau

This meatless variation of the typical pork laulau was used in the last week of the Hawaii Health Program which was a vegetarian week. ◌ঝ

1 lb.	Sweet potatoes
1 lb.	Taro
8 - 12	Ti leaves
1 lb.	Taro *(lu'au)* **leaves,** *(if unavailable, use spinach leaves)*
	Salt, to taste

Cut taro stems from taro leaves. Wash taro leaves. Separate into four portions.

Taro and taro leaves must be cooked properly. Do NOT eat raw. For more information see pages 55 and 189.

Wash and scrub taro and sweet potatoes thoroughly until clean. Peel and cut into 1/2" cubes.

Place portions of sweet potatoes and taro on taro leaves; salt to taste. Wrap in ti leaves. Steam in pressure cooker for 20 to 25 minutes or until done.

Variation:

You can cook other vegetables in this manner such as carrots, white potatoes, squash, etc.

In case you don't already know, the ti leaf is the traditional laulau wrapper, but is itself inedible.

Makes 4 portions. *(1 portion = 264 calories, 0.8 gram fat, 10% protein, 88% carbohydrates, 2% fat)*

Nishime

This is a traditional Japanese stew-like dish that is low fat and was one of the favorite dishes on both the HawaiiDiet™ Study and the Program. ৫

2 strips	Konbu *(dried)*
4 pieces	Mushrooms *(dried)*
2	Konyaku,* sliced
3	Aburage*
1 C	Turnip
2 C	Japanese taro
1 C	Bamboo shoots
1 C	Carrots
1 C	Burdock root
1 tsp.	Peanut oil
1-1/2 C	Vegetable broth
1/4 C	Tamari
1/3 C	Sugar

Soak konbu and mushrooms in water until soft, about 10 minutes.

Wash and scrub Japanese taro thoroughly until clean. Peel and cut into 1-1/2" pieces.

Cut konbu, konyaku, aburage, turnip, bamboo shoots, and carrots into 1-1/2" pieces. Cut burdock root into 1/4"-thick diagonal slices and soak in water until used.

Tie konbu into knots leaving 1" apart. Cut between knots.

In a saucepan, add peanut oil, vegetable broth, mushrooms, konbu, konyaku, and bamboo shoots. Cover and cook for 10 minutes. Add tamari and sugar; cook for 5 minutes. Add turnip, carrots, and burdock root and cook for 15 minutes. Add taro and cook until taro is fork tender. Toss in aburage and serve.

Makes 4 portions.

Taro must be cooked properly. Do NOT eat raw. (See page 55 for more information.)

* *Konyaku is a chewy product made from yam flour. Aburage is fried tofu skin, also used for cone sushi. Both are available where Japanese foods are sold.*

Potato, Eggplant & Zucchini Pie

3	Red potatoes, peeled
1/2 lb.	Asian Eggplant
2 small	Zucchini
	Garlic powder

SAUCE:

1 large	Onion, peeled and thinly sliced
2 cloves	Garlic, chopped
1/4 C	Parsley *(fresh)*, finely chopped
1 can	Stewed tomatoes *(14 oz.)*
2 Tbsp.	Basil *(fresh)* or 2 tsp. basil *(dried)*
1 tsp.	Oregano leaves *(dried)*
1/2 tsp.	Salt
1/2 tsp.	Black pepper, freshly ground
	Canola oil nonstick spray

Sauce:

Spray saucepan with nonstick spray. Sauté onions and garlic until onions are translucent. Add tomatoes, parsley, basil, oregano, salt, and pepper. Simmer until sauce thickens, about 30 minutes.

Pie:

Cook potatoes in water for 20 minutes. Drain, cool, and slice into 1/8"-thick slices.

Trim the ends of the zucchini and slice into 1/4" lengthwise slices.

Peel and cut eggplant into 1/4" thick slices.

Spray baking sheet with nonstick spray. Arrange zucchini and eggplant slices on sheet, sprinkle with garlic powder, and bake at 400°F. for 10 minutes, turning once.

Spray 8" square baking pan with nonstick spray. Lay potatoes on bottom. Top with some of sauce. Layer eggplant next and top with more sauce. Top with zucchini and spread remaining sauce over zucchini.

Bake at 350°F. for 30 to 40 minutes.

Makes 10 portions. *(1 portion = 60 calories, 0.4 gram fat, 10% protein, 84% carbohydrates, 6% fat)*

Vegetarian Eight Treasures

This is a great traditional Chinese dish that has continued through all our programs because of its popularity. ∞

2	Bean curd cakes
1 tsp.	Peanut oil
1 medium	Cucumber
1 medium	Carrot
1 can	Water chestnuts
1/2 lb.	Chinese peas
2 tsp.	Chili paste
2 Tbsp.	Sweet bean sauce
3 Tbsp.	Soy sauce
1-1/2 Tbsp.	Sugar
1 Tbsp.	Rice wine
1-1/2 Tbsp.	Water
1/4 C	Peanuts, unsalted and dry roasted

Soak bean curd in hot water for one hour. Drain by placing bean curd between paper towels. Place a light weight on wrapped bean curd for 1 hour. Cut into 1/2" pieces.

Dice the cucumber and carrots in 1/2" pieces. Steam for 8 minutes.

Drain and dice water chestnuts.

In a skillet or wok water-sauté carrot, water chestnuts, bean curd, peas, and cucumber for 1 to 2 minutes. Remove from skillet or wok.

In the same pan, stir fry peanut oil and chili paste for about 10 seconds. Add sweet bean and soy sauces, sugar, rice wine, and water until sauce begins to thicken. Add the cooked vegetables and peanuts and toss lightly until mixed. Serve.

Most of the fat in this recipe comes from the peanuts, so go easy on them to keep the fat content down.

Makes 6 portions. *(1 portion = 142 calories, 5.6 grams fat, 21% protein, 44% carbohydrates, 34% fat)*

Vegetarian Chop Suey

This is a Chinese-style stir fry which could be high fat except that we keep the use of oil down to a minimum and make use of the water, soy sauce (tamari), and arrowroot as the sauté medium. ∝

1/2	Onion, thinly sliced
1 C	Celery, thinly sliced
2 C	Chop suey mix *(mainly bean sprouts, carrots, a little celery, and a little watercress)*
1 C	Water chestnuts, thinly sliced
1/2 C	Snowpeas
1 tsp.	Peanut oil
1/4 C	Water
1/2 tsp.	Salt
1/4 tsp.	Black pepper
1/4 tsp.	Salt
1 tsp.	Tamari
1-1/2 tsp.	Arrowroot, add water to make paste

Mix peanut oil, water, 1/2 teaspoon salt, and black pepper in a wok or skillet. Add onion, celery, chop suey mix, and water chestnuts. Cover and cook for 10 to 15 minutes. During the last 5 minutes, add the snow peas.

Drain sauce from vegetables. Measure out liquid, adding water, if necessary, to make 1-1/4 cups. *(As you stir fry, liquid evaporates.)* Place liquid in a saucepan and add 1/4 teaspoon salt, tamari, and arrowroot paste. When thickened, pour back over vegetables, toss, and serve.

Makes 4 portions. *(1 portion = 84 calories, 1.4 grams fat, 13% protein, 73% carbohydrates, 14% fat)*

Thai Vegetable Curry

This is a curry that has a slightly exotic Thai flavor to it. For something more familiar try my "Local Style Curry Stew" in the Eat More, Weigh Less® Cookbook on page 206." ◌

1 tsp.	Canola oil
2	Shallots
2 cloves	Garlic, minced
2-3 Tbsp.	Curry powder
1/2 tsp.	Turmeric
1 tsp.	Chili paste, ground
2 Tbsp.	Soy sauce
1 stalk	Lemon grass *(use blender)*
1" piece	Ginger *(fresh)*
1/4 C	Coconut milk *(low fat)*
2-3/4 C	Rice milk
1 Tbsp.	Coconut extract
1/2 tsp.	Salt
3 Tbsp.	Light brown sugar
2	Carrots, peeled and sliced 1/2" thick
1 lb.	Russet potatoes, peeled and cubed into 1" pieces
1/2	Onion, chopped
1/2 head	Cauliflower, cut into 1" pieces
2 C	Green beans, sliced diagonally
2	Tomatoes, cut into thin wedges
3	Kaffir lime leaves, slivered
10	Thai basil leaves *(fresh)*

In a large saucepan, heat canola oil and sauté shallot, garlic, curry powder, turmeric and chili paste for 1 to 2 minutes. Add soy sauce, lemon grass, and ginger and stir for 30 seconds. Add rice milk, coconut milk, coconut extract, salt, and brown sugar. Bring to a boil. Add carrots, potatoes, onions, and cauliflower and cook until almost tender. Add green beans and tomatoes and cook for approximately 3 minutes. Stir in lime and basil leaves before serving. Remove from heat and serve.

Makes 5 portions. *(1 portion = 246 calories, 7.4 grams fat, 14% protein, 60% carbohydrates, 26% fat)*

Tofu with Tomato Sauce

2 blocks	Tofu *(firm)*, cut into 1/2" slices
1/2 tsp.	Salt
1 tsp.	White pepper
2 medium	Maui onions, thinly sliced
2 Tbsp.	Vegetable oil
1 Tbsp.	Tomato paste
3 cloves	Garlic, minced
1/2 C	White wine
1/2 C	Water
2 Tbsp.	Chicken-flavored boullion *(powdered)*
1	Bay leaf
3	Tomatoes *(ripe)*
	All purpose flour
	Chinese parsley, minced *(garnish)*

In a colander, drain tofu and sprinkle with salt and pepper.

Sauté onion in 1 tablespoon of oil until golden brown. Stir in garlic and tomato paste and cook for 2 minutes. Add wine and bring to boil, then add water and boullion, bay leaf, and tomatoes.

Coat tofu with flour. In another pan, sauté tofu in 1 tablespoon of oil until golden brown. Gently place tofu in tomato sauce and simmer until sauce thickens. Season to taste and garnish with minced parsley.

Makes 4 portions. *(1 portion = 175 calories, 7.8 grams fat, 33% protein, 27% carbohydrates, 40% fat)*

Tofu Stir Fry

3 cubes	Chicken-flavored bouillon cubes
1-1/2 C	Water
3/4 C	Dry sherry
3 Tbsp.	Cornstarch
4 Tbsp.	Vegetarian stir fry sauce
5 Tbsp.	Soy sauce
3 tsp.	Ginger, minced
3 C	Carrots, sliced
6 cloves	Garlic, minced
9 C	Broccoli, cut into bite-size pieces
18 oz.	Tofu, cut in 1" cubes
3 Tbsp.	Sesame seeds, toasted
	Chinese parsley

Dissolve 3 cubes of chicken-flavored bouillon cubes in 1-1/2 cups of water. Add sherry, cornstarch, and soy and stir fry sauce. Set aside.

Water-sauté garlic and ginger for 2 minutes. Add carrots and cook for 4 minutes, then add broccoli and cook until tender.

Push vegetable to the side and stir in sauce until it thickens. Add and cook tofu for 3 minutes stirring constantly. Place in serving platter and garnish with sesame seeds and Chinese parsley.

Makes 8 portions. *(1 portion = 189 calories, 4.8 grams fat, 27% protein, 49% carbohydrates, 24% fat)*

Sweet & Sour Tofu with Chinese Peas & Mushrooms

12 oz.	Tofu, cut into 1/2" cubes
1 C	Chinese peas
1 can	Bamboo shoots *(medium-sized can)*
2	Chinese mushroom *(dried)*
1 medium	Onion, sliced
2	Pineapple slices
2 cloves	Garlic, minced

SWEET SOUR SAUCE:

1 Tbsp.	Ketchup
2 Tbsp.	Tamari
1/2 C	Pineapple syrup
3 Tbsp.	Vinegar
1/4 C	Brown sugar
1 Tbsp.	Cornstarch, dissolved in 1/4 C water

Soak dried mushrooms in water.

Wash and remove strings around Chinese pea pods.

Cut bamboo shoots lengthwise into halves, then crosswise into 1/8" slices.

Drain mushrooms and slice. Slice onion. Cut pineapple slices into 1/8's.

In a small saucepan, add sweet sour sauce ingredients and simmer until ready to pour over stir-fried mixture.

~

Water-sauté garlic and onion. Add bamboo shoots, mushrooms, Chinese peas, pineapple, and tofu. Stir fry over medium high heat for approximately 2 minutes.

Pour sweet sour sauce over vegetables and mix in. Serve.

Makes 6 portions. *(1 portion = 207 calories, 2.6 grams fat, 13% protein, 76% carbohydrates, 11% fat)*

Yaki Somen

"Somen" are very thin noodles which you can find in any Asian grocery, or in the Asian section of your local super-market or health food store. If they are unavailable where you live, you may substitute regular soba noodles, which are larger, or capellini (angel hair pasta). ❧

1 pkg.	Somen noodles *(14 oz.)*
1 tsp.	Sesame oil *(for stir fry)*
	Teriyaki sauce, to taste
1 C	Carrots, julienned
1 C	Cabbage, sliced thin or chopped thin
1 C	Mung bean sprouts
1/2 C	Broccoli flowerettes
1/4 C	Onions, sliced thin

Precook somen, soba, or other type of pasta until tender, according to package instructions. When done, drain, rinse to remove starch water, and set aside. While it is cooking, julienne or otherwise prepare vegetables.

Preheat a large wok. When hot, add sesame oil *(it should sizzle)*. Then toss in all vegetables, stir frequently until they are crispy-tender. Add somen, then add teri-yaki sauce, to taste, continuing to stir fry until the dish is reheated throughout. *Be careful not to overcook at this point, or the pasta will lose its firmness.*

Serve to individual dishes. Cooking time about 15 minutes, not counting precooked pasta time.

Makes 2 portions as an entrée, 4 portions as a side dish. *(1 portion as an entrée = 794 calories., 4.3 gm fat, 13% protein, 82% carbohydrates, 5% fat)   (1 portion as side dish = 397 calories., 2.1 gm fat, 13% protein, 82% carbohydrates, 5% fat)*

Avalon's Pasta Gerry

Chef Mark Ellman shares a recipe from his Avalon Restaurant at Lahaina, Maui. This pasta has an interesting combination of flavors I think you will enjoy, and it is easy to prepare. ∞

1 tsp.	Ginger, chopped
1 tsp.	Garlic, chopped
1 tsp.	Onion, chopped
1 tsp.	Extra virgin olive oil
1/2 tsp.	Sesame oil
1/2 tsp.	Fermented black beans, chopped
1/8 C	Shiitake mushrooms, sliced
1 tsp.	Mint *(fresh)*, chopped
1 tsp.	Basil *(fresh)*, chopped
1 tsp.	Cilantro *(fresh)*, chopped
1 C	Tomatoes *(fresh or high quality canned)*, chopped
1/2 C	White wine or vegetable broth

Sauté first 10 ingredients for 5 minutes. Add tomatoes and wine or vegetable broth. Cook for 5 minutes. Add more fresh herbs. Serve with your favorite pasta.

Makes 8 portions. *(1 portion with 4 oz. pasta = 200 calories, 3.0 grams fat, 14% protein, 70% carbohydrates, 16% fat)*

Tomato, White Bean & Spinach Pasta

1 tsp.	Olive oil or cooking spray
1/4 C	Garlic, coarsely minced
1/4 C	Basil leaves *(fresh)*, slivered, or 2 tsp. dried
2 large	Roma tomatoes *(ripe)* or 1 large tomato, chopped
1 can	Tomatoes *(15 oz., no salt added, ready cut, peeled)*, or tomatoes *(15 oz., Italian recipe, stewed)*, chopped
1 C	White beans *(Great Northern or cannellini)*, cooked; rinsed and drained, if canned
1 C	Spinach leaves *(fresh)*, washed thoroughly, dried, and finely shredded
1 tsp.	Black pepper or 1/4 tsp. hot red pepper flakes, crushed; or to taste
1 pkg.	Penne or mostaccioli pasta

In a large, nonstick saucepan over medium heat add olive oil, garlic, basil, and pepper. Cook about 2 minutes, stirring to make sure garlic doesn't overcook.

Add ripe and canned tomatoes. Cover and bring to a boil; reduce heat and simmer for 8 to 10 minutes. Add beans and cook, stirring for 2 minutes. Add 1 to 2 tablespoons vegetable broth or water if sauce is too thick.

Cook the pasta according to directions; drain. Immediately toss pasta with tomato-bean sauce and spinach. Season to taste and serve. Makes 8 portions. *(1 portion = 97 calories, 1.3 grams fat, 18% protein, 71% carbohydrates, 11% fat)*

Mushroom Marinara Sauce for Pasta*

1/4 C	Red wine
2 oz.	Mushrooms *(dried, any type)*
2 cloves	Garlic, peeled and pressed
1 large	Onion, sliced thinly
2 Tbsp.	Basil *(fresh)*
1 Tbsp.	Rosemary *(fresh)*
5 Tbsp.	Parsley *(fresh)*
2 tsp.	Oregano *(fresh)*
3 C	Plum tomatoes, canned with juices
	Salt, to taste
	Black pepper, freshly ground, to taste

Break the herbs apart. Twist the leaves or stems into 1/8" pieces or slightly smaller. *This is the best way to release the full flavor of herbs.* Put aside.

Soak dried mushrooms in 1 cup hot water for 15 to 20 minutes. Drain and strain the mushrooms, reserving the soaking liquid. Rinse and chop the mushrooms.

Heat a large nonstick skillet. Water-sauté garlic cloves, onion, then quickly add parsley, oregano, rosemary, and basil. When the herbs begin to wilt, add tomatoes with juice and mushroom soaking water. Bring to a boil, turn down heat, add salt and pepper to taste and let simmer for about 10 minutes.

Makes 6 portions. *(1 portion = 69 calories, 0.6 grams fat, 16% protein, 76% carbohydrates, 7% fat)*

* From **Dr. Shintani's Eat More, Weigh Less® Cookbook**, page 130

Maui Tacos' Black Bean Burrito

One of my assistants asserts that caffeine and newsprint make a complete protein. This is not so. However, rice and beans, the daily fare of Latin Americans, do make a healthy combination. Add some potatoes and enjoy this hearty burrito recipe contributed by Chef Mark Ellman of Avalon and Maui Tacos restaurants. If you want this made for you, go to one of the Maui Tacos locations in Napili, Lahaina, Kihei, Kahului, Hilo, and Honolulu. ✑

12 oz.	Rice, cooked or Spanish rice
5 small	Potatoes
1/2	Onion, chopped
1 Tbsp.	Garlic *(granulated)*
1 tsp.	Salt
1 can	Black beans *(16 oz.),* or cooked *(page 215)*
5	Tortillas *(12")*
8 oz.	Lettuce, shredded
7 oz.	Salsa or Maui Tacos' Pineapple Tomatillo Salsa *(page 96)*
4 oz.	Maui Tacos' Guacamole *(page 97)*

Wash and peel potatoes. Place in saucepan and water to cover. Add salt. Boil potatoes for 35 to 40 minutes. Drain water and cube into 1/2" cubes and set aside.

Water-sauté onion and granulated garlic until translucent. Add black beans, potatoes, and rice. Gently mix together until combined.

Lay out tortillas on a flat surface. Layer the filling in the following order: black bean-potato-rice mixture, lettuce, salsa, and guacamole. Fold tortilla over layers, envelope fashion.

Makes 5 portions. *(1 portion with guacamole = 440 calories, 4.9 grams fat, 13% protein, 77% carbohydrates, 10% fat)   (1 portion without guacamole = 416 calories, 2.7 grams fat, 13% protein, 81% carbohydrates, 6% fat)*

Dick Algire's Lazy Enchiladas

Television newsman Dick Algire, who contributed this recipe, says: "I call these 'Lazy Enchiladas' because the sauce and filling are cooked in the same pot and there is no baking time. With tomato on the inside, it has a nice creamy texture that I missed when giving up cheese. The spices are approximate because I don't measure; just taste until it's right." ભ

1 medium	Onion, chopped
1/2 medium	Red/green pepper, chopped
2 cloves	Garlic, minced *(bottled)*
9-10 medium	Mushrooms, sliced thinly
1 can	Stewed tomatoes *(15 oz.)*, with juice
1/2 C	Corn kernels *(frozen)*, thawed
1 can	Black beans *(15 oz.)*, rinsed
1/2 tsp.	Cinnamon
1/2 tsp.	Oregano, or to taste
2 Tbsp.	Chili powder, or to taste
1-2 tsp.	Cumin *(ground)*, or to taste
pinch	Cayenne, or to taste
4 medium	Flour tortillas

Water-sauté onion, pepper, and garlic until onion is translucent. Add spices and let them coat the onion mixture. Add mushrooms and let cook briefly for 1 to 2 minutes. Add can of stewed tomatoes and bring to a simmer, reduce heat and simmer for 10 minutes. Add corn and simmer for 10 more minutes. Add beans, and simmer for 5 minutes.

Warm tortillas so they are pliable, and with a slotted spoon scoop mixture in tortilla, roll, and place on dinner plate. With tablespoon, take liquid and pour over tortillas. Repeat until done.

Simmering times are approximate, but essentially you want to let it cook so the flavors have combined, but not to reduce to a true stew. It should look like a soupy stew, so that you have liquid to put on tortillas.

Makes 4 portions. *(1 portion = 316 calories, 3.5 grams fat, 18% protein, 72% carbohydrates, 10% fat)*

Side Dishes
'Ono Taro Tops

Taro (lu'au) leaves are very high in calcium, iron, and vitamins. They are one of the most nutritious foods of Hawaii. ↷

1 pkg.	Taro *(lu'au)* leaves *(1 lb., precooked)*
1 whole	Hawaiian taro
1 small	Onion, chopped
1 piece	Ginger, minced
1 clove	Garlic, minced
1 tsp.	Hawaiian salt
	Dash of pepper
2-3 Tbsp.	Coconut milk
1/4 Tbsp.	Soy milk

Cook taro and cut up in pieces. *(See page 55 for taro cooking instructions and precautions.)*

Wash taro leaves; remove stems, and chop into large pieces. In a saucepan cover leaves with enough water to let them boil freely. Simmer for 20 minutes; drain and set aside. *(See next page for taro leaf information and precautions.)*

In a saucepan, water-sauté ginger, garlic, onion, and Hawaiian salt. Add coconut milk, soy milk, taro leaves, and taro. Bring to a boil and remove from heat immediately. Serve warm.

Makes 4 portions. *(1 portion = 239 calories, 3.2 grams fat, 8% protein, 81% carbohydrates, 11% fat)*

If your skin gets itchy after contact with raw taro or taro leaves, make a paste out of baking soda and water, then spread on affected area until itching disappears, then wash off.

Taro leaves contain microscopic calcium oxalate crystals, which are like fine needles and must be broken down by cooking. Taro leaves that are not cooked well will cause an unpleasant itchiness in the throat when eaten.

Wakame with Mixed Vegetables

Wakame with mixed vegetables is another high calcium dish primarily because of the seaweed (wakame). ℘

2-1/2 oz.	Wakame, dried
5 C	Daikon, sliced
5 C	Carrots, sliced
5 C	Cauliflower, cut
5 C	Turnips, sliced
8 Tbsp.	Soy sauce *(low sodium)*
	Water
	Green onions *(garnish)*

Rinse and soak wakame. Slice into large pieces.

Put other vegetables in a large soup pot and half cover with water. Bring to a boil, cover, and reduce heat to low, simmering until the vegetables are almost cooked. Add wakame and low-sodium soy sauce to taste until the vegetables are cooked.

Serve one cup in a bowl and garnish with green onions.

Makes 20 portions. *(1 portion = 47 calories, 0.3 grams fat, 17% protein, 78% carbohydrates, 5% fat)*

Wakame with Carrots

Wakame with carrots is a variation on the previous recipe that is not only high in calcium but also in beta carotene and the family of carotenoids which are powerful antioxidants. ♋

2 oz.	Wakame *(dried)*
4 C	Carrots, cut into large chunks
	Water to cover vegetables
2 Tbsp.	Soy sauce *(low sodium)*
	Cilantro, scallions, or parsley *(garnish)*

Rinse and soak wakame. Slice into large pieces.

Put the carrots in a pot and add water to half cover the carrots. Bring to a boil, cover, and reduce heat to low. Simmer until the carrots are nearly cooked, about 20 to 30 minutes. Then add the soy sauce and wakame. Simmer until carrots are done. Garnish.

Makes 4 portions. *(1 portion = 60 calories, 0.3 gram fat, 14% protein, 82% carbohydrates, 4% fat)*

Wakame Namasu

"Namasu" is a traditional Japanese dish which literally means "raw with vinegar," so this is a dish of raw vegetables with a sweet vinegar dressing. You can actually use this preparation with just about any raw vegetables for a great, tasty, no-fat meal. Wakame, which is a tender, leafy sea vegetable, lends itself well with this dish and is also high in calcium. ❧

1/4 C	Vinegar
3 Tbsp.	Honey
1/2 tsp.	Salt
1/2 tsp.	Ginger *(fresh)*, **grated**
	Juice from 1/2 lemon or lime
1 pkg.	**Wakame** *(1 oz.)*
1	**Carrot**

Combine vinegar, honey, salt, ginger, and lemon or lime juice. Set aside.

Julienne carrot and sprinkle with salt. Let stand for about 30 minutes. Rinse and squeeze water from carrots.

Soak wakame in cold water just until hydrated. Squeeze out excess water. Combine wakame, carrots, and sauce. Serve.

Makes 4 portions. *(1 portion = 64 calories, 0.1 gram fat, 3% protein, 96% carbohydrates, 1% fat)*

Ginger Mustard Cabbage with Konbu*

Mustard cabbage and konbu (seaweed) are both excellent sources of calcium and this is a versatile side dish to complement most entrées. ∾

2 lbs.	Mustard cabbage
1 Tbsp.	Sea salt
1/3 C	Konbu *(dried)*, cut in 1/2" strips
1/3 C	Barley malt
1/4 C	Soy sauce *(low sodium)*
1/4 C	Rice vinegar
1 Tbsp.	Sesame seeds, toasted
1 Tbsp.	Ginger root, minced

Chop cabbage, add salt, and let stand for 30 minutes.

Wash konbu and soak until soft. Drain and discard liquid, then cut into 1/2" lengths.

In a saucepan, mix barley malt and soy sauce. Heat until sugar dissolves. Add vinegar then konbu while still hot.

Cool the sauce a little, then mix in the rest of ingredients. Transfer to a storage container and let sit overnight in refrigerator to blend flavors.

Makes four *(8-ounce)* portions. *(1 serving = 85 calories, 1.6 gm. fat, 15% protein, 75% carbohydrates, 10% fat)*

* From **Dr. Shintani's Eat More, Weigh Less® Cookbook**, page 269

Mock Crabmeat Sauce Over Broccoli

This was very highly rated by the participants on the HawaiiDiet™ Study and on the Hawaii Health Program.
CR

1-1/2 lb.	Broccoli
1 cake	Tofu
1 tsp.	Sesame oil
1 tsp.	Peanut oil
1-1/2 tsp.	Garlic, minced
2 tsp.	Ginger *(fresh)*, minced
5 Tbsp.	White table wine
2 tsp.	Salt
1/2 C	Water
1/2 tsp.	Sugar
1/4 tsp.	White pepper, freshly ground
2	Egg whites, beaten
1-1/2 tsp.	Cornstarch, mixed with 1 Tbsp. water
3 Tbsp.	Carrot, minced

Wash and cut broccoli flowerettes and stems. Cut stems in 1" diagonal pieces. Steam broccoli in steamer for 3 minutes.

Mash tofu with fork and add 1/2 teaspoon sesame oil.

Heat wok or skillet to high and add peanut oil. Add garlic and ginger and cook for 10 seconds. Add broccoli, 3-1/2 tablespoons of wine, 1-1/2 teaspoon salt, sesame oil and stir fry for 1 minute. Remove and set on platter. Clean the wok or skillet.

Reheat wok to high and add mashed tofu and stir fry for 30 seconds. Add 1/2 cup of water, 1-1/2 tablespoons wine, 1/2 teaspoon salt, 1/2 teaspoon sugar, 1/4 teaspoon pepper and 2 beaten egg whites. Cook for 20 seconds. Slowly add cornstarch mixture, stirring constantly until sauce thickens.

Pour mixture over broccoli and sprinkle minced carrot over broccoli. Serve immediately.

Makes 4 portions. *(1 portion = 120 calories, 4.1 grams fat, 30% protein, 40% carbohydrates, 30% fat)*

Steamed Garlic Broccoli

This is a simple, high-calcium dish that can be used as a side dish to just about any entrée. In addition to being high in calcium, broccoli is a "cruicferous vegetable," which means it is loaded with anti-cancer nutrients such as beta carotene, indole amines, and fiber. Steamed Garlic Broccoli was served on the Hawaii Health Program as well as the Hawaii-Diet™ Study. ❧

1 bunch	Broccoli, chopped
1 clove	Garlic, minced
1/2 C	Water
sprinkle	Sesame seed, roasted or sesame salt

Wash and chop the broccoli, separating the stems and flowerettes. Place the broccoli stems in a 1-1/2-quart saucepan with the water and garlic; cover and steam for 4 minutes. Uncover and stir the stems, arrange the flowerettes on top, then cover and steam for another 4 minutes.

Serve with a sprinkling of roasted sesame seeds or sesame salt *(gomasio).*

Makes 4 portions. *(1 portion = 28 calories, 0.3 gram fat, 33% protein, 59% carbohydrates, 8% fat)*

Broccoli With Mustard Sauce

This is another simple, high-calcium dish. ❧

1 bunch	Broccoli
1/2 cup	Rice vinegar *(seasoned)*
2 tsp.	Mustard *(Stone ground or Dijon-style)*
1-2 cloves	Garlic, pressed or minced

Break broccoli into bite-sized flowerettes. Peel the stems and slice them into 1/4" thick rounds. Steam until just tender, about 3 minutes. While broccoli is steaming, whisk the remaining ingredients in a serving bowl. Add the steamed broccoli and toss to mix. Serve immediately.

Makes 4 portions. *(1 portion = 36 calories, 0.4 gram fat, 28% protein, 64% carbohydrates, 8% fat)*

Spicy Szechuan Eggplant*

1-1/2 lbs.   Eggplant, peeled and cut into 3" strips
1 C   Chinese wood ear fungus *(or shiitake,*
             straw, or other mushrooms), soaked
             and sliced into strips
             Canola oil cooking spray

GARLIC SAUCE:

1/4 C	Soy sauce
1 Tbsp.	Honey
1 Tbsp.	Distilled white vinegar
1 Tbsp.	Cornstarch
2 red	Chili peppers, minced
2 slices	Ginger, minced
2 cloves	Garlic, minced

Mix all sauce ingredients and set aside.

Spray pan with oil. Sauté eggplant over medium heat until golden brown, about 5 minutes.

Combine sauce with eggplant and fungus. Cook for 1 minute.

Makes 4 portions. *(1 portion = 97 calories, 1.0 gram fat, 15% protein, 79% carbohydrates, 5% fat)*

* *From* **Dr. Shintani's Eat More, Weigh Less® Cookbook**, *page 220*

Herbed Asparagus*

Tarragon and dill are just the touch that adds flavor to this low-fat dish. ⁂

1 lb.	Asparagus *(fresh)*
4 Tbsp.	Water, for steamer
1 Tbsp.	Vegetable broth
3 - 4	Green onions, thinly sliced
1 Tbsp.	Tarragon *(fresh)*, chopped
1 Tbsp.	Dill *(fresh)* or 1 tsp. *(dried)*
	Sea salt, to taste

Steam asparagus until tender, about 5 minutes *(do not overcook)*. Rinse, drain, and serve to plate.

In a small skillet, sauté scallions for 1 to 2 minutes in vegetable broth. Add the tarragon, dill, and salt to skillet. Add water if it begins to dry out.

Cook for 1 to 2 minutes until liquid reduces slightly. Use as sauce over asparagus. Serve warm or cool.

Makes 4 portions *(1 portion = 34 calories, 0.7 gram fat, 38% protein, 43% carbohydrates, 19% fat)*

* *From **Dr. Shintani's Eat More, Weigh Less® Cookbook**, page 215*

*Melt-In-Your-Mouth Kabocha Squash**

See Eat More, Weigh Less® Diet *book and* Eat More, Weigh Less® Cookbook *for more squash recipes.* ❧

1   Kabocha or acorn squash

Cut the kabocha squash into 4" squares or cleaned acorn squash in quarters. Place on a baking pan with a tiny bit of water and bake at 350° F. until tender, about an hour.

Remember, you can eat the skin and all, so wash it all before you prepare it.

Makes 2 portions. *(1 portion = 115 calories, 0.3 grams fat, 7% protein, 91% carbohydrates, 2% fat)*

Variation:

For a little zing, try adding a tablespoon of miso and a teaspoon of sweetener such as barley malt.

* *From* **Dr. Shintani's Eat More, Weigh Less® Cookbook**, *page 230*

Staples

Roasted Potatoes

This dish brings out the full flavor of potatoes and yet limits the fat to under 2 grams and less than 10% of calories as compared to typical fried potatoes (which would be about 8 grams of fat and 48% fat by calories per serving). ∞

1-1/2 lb.	Red potatoes, unpeeled
1 head	Garlic, roasted
1/4 C	Rosemary, chopped
	Salt, to taste
	Black pepper, freshly ground, to taste
	Olive oil cooking spray

Preheat oven to 375° F.

Cut potatoes in halves and place in baking pan. Cut ends of garlic and spread over roasted potatoes. Spray olive oil and sprinkle with rosemary. Cover pan and bake for 20 minutes. Remove cover and roast for 10 to 15 minutes. Season with salt and pepper.

Makes 3 portions. *(1 portion = 273 calories, 1.2 grams fat, 9% protein, 87% carbohydrates, 4% fat)*

Teriyaki Potatoes

For a change of pace in potatoes, try this East-West variation that combines great tastes of two worlds – baked potatoes with "teriyaki" taste. ∝

1/2 C	Soy sauce
3 Tbsp.	Brown sugar
3 cloves	Garlic, mashed
1 piece	Ginger, 1", mashed
2 stalks	Green onion, chopped
1 tsp.	Sesame oil
	Black pepper, to taste
2 lbs.	Red potatoes, peeled and quartered

Preheat oven to 375° F.

In a bowl combine soy sauce, brown sugar, garlic, ginger, green onion, sesame oil, and black pepper; mix well.

Place the potatoes in this same bowl and marinate overnight, stirring occasionally.

Line a baking pan with aluminum foil and place the marinated potatoes in the middle of the pan.

Bake for 25 to 30 minutes, basting with the marinade. Broil the potatoes the last 10 minutes for a crispy texture.

Makes 8 portions. *(1 portion = 136 calories, 0.7 gram fat, 10% protein, 85% carbohydrates, 5% fat)*

Chestnut Stuffing

Great for holidays or anytime that you want an alternative to mashed potatoes or other starchy staples. ↷

1/2 C	Onion, minced
1-2 stalks	Celery
1	Apple, minced
8-10	Water chestnuts, chopped
1 tsp.	Salt
1 tsp.	Sage
1 tsp.	Thyme
1/2 tsp.	Pepper
5 C	Whole wheat bread and white bread, cubed and mixed together
1/2 lb.	Chestnuts, boiled *(breadfruit, in season, can be used)*
3/4 C	Chicken-flavored broth

Water-sauté onions, celery, apple, and water chestnuts. When onions are translucent add salt, sage, thyme, and pepper. Add bread cubes and chestnuts, alternating with chicken flavored broth.

Makes 10 portions. *(1 portion = 179 calories, 2.3 grams fat, 12% protein, 77% carbohydrates, 11% fat)*

Basmati Brown Rice*

This is an excellent brown rice for people who are accustomed to white rice and are trying to replace it with a brown rice. I like basmati brown rice because it has a rich, nutty aroma to it so that it takes on a character of its own even without adding spices. I comment more about it in Tip #6 in Dr. Shintani's Eat More, Weigh Less® Cookbook. ❧

2 C	Basmati *(or other brown rice)*
3-1/2 to 4 C	Water
2 pinches	Sea salt

Gently wash rice until water rinses clear. If possible, soak for 2 to 6 hours.

Place rice in a 2-quart pot *(stainless steel is best)*. Cover with water and add sea salt. Cover, bring to a boil, reduce heat then simmer for 45 minutes to one hour. *(Do not uncover rice while cooking.)* When done, remove from burner and let sit for 10 more minutes before serving.

Makes 6 portions. *(1 portion (1 cup) = 216 calories, 1.8 grams fat, 9% protein, 83% carbohydrates, 7% fat)*

*You may also prepare basmati in a rice cooker or pressure cooker. See Tip #7 and Tip #8 in **Dr. Shintani's Eat More, Weigh Less® Cookbook.***

* From **Dr. Shintani's Eat More, Weigh Less® Cookbook**, page 57

Rice Cooker Brown Rice

Everyone who is in a hurry should own a rice cooker and learn how to make rice in it. You just measure out the water, usually 2 cups of water for each cup of rice. I like to add a pinch of sea salt. Then just press the button and forget it until the bell goes off and its done! ∽

2 C	Water
1 C	Brown rice
pinch	Sea salt

Rinse and drain rice. Place rice, water and salt in rice cooker. Follow directions provided by the manufacturer.

Makes 3 portions. *(1 portion = 216 calories, 1.8 grams fat, 9% protein, 83% carbohydrates, 7% fat)*

Pressure Cooked Brown Rice*

This is my preferred method of cooking brown rice. Pressure cooking is fast and it seals in flavor and nutrients. ca

RATIO:

1-1/3 to 1-3/4 C	Water per cup of rice
1 C	Brown rice
pinch	Sea salt

Rinse rice. Soak 2 to 6 hours, if you have time. Rice will take a little longer to cook if not presoaked.

Place rice and water into a pressure cooker *(stainless steel if possible)*. Add salt, cover with lid as directed by manufacturer of pressure cooker.

Bring to pressure on high heat then lower to low heat and cook for 30 to 40 minutes. Let pressure come down, then let stand for 5 to 10 minutes, stir and serve.

Makes 3 portions. *(1 portion = 216 calories, 1.8 grams fat, 9% protein, 83% carbohydrates, 7% fat)*

* *From **Dr. Shintani's Eat More, Weigh Less® Cookbook**, page 60*

Gandule Rice

This is a dish that everyone should try at least once. It is a Puerto Rican dish that is very low in fat and has a zesty flavor. It was probably the best liked recipe in our cooking classes. ♋

4 C	Rice, uncooked, washed, and drained
2 C	Gandule beans or 1 can gandule beans (15 oz.), drained
1	Bell pepper, chopped
1 large	Onion, diced
2 bunches	Cilantro, chopped
3-4 cloves	Garlic
2-3 stalks	Celery, diced
1 can	Tomato sauce (8 oz.)
1 env.	Goya powder or chili powder
	Salt, to taste or Vegesol®
1 tsp.	Cumin
1 tsp.	Oregano
1-2 tsp.	Extra virgin olive oil
3 C	Vegetarian chicken-flavored broth
	Olives, sliced
	Chinese parsley

In a large pot, sauté all vegetables in olive oil. Add seasonings, goya powder. Add gandules and sauté for another 5 minutes. Add broth and tomato sauce and bring to a boil. Taste and add more salt or seasoning if needed.

At this point this dish can be cooked on the stove or transferred to a crock pot. See crock pot instructions below.

Stir in rice and bring to a boil. Cook for about 2 minutes over high heat, stirring occasionally. Reduce heat to low. Cover and simmer for about an hour. The mixture should be the consistency of porridge.

Garnish with olives and Chinese parsley.

To Prepare In Crock Pot:

Transfer to the crock pot and lower heat to simmer. Cover pot and cook for 2 hours. After 30 minutes stir rice mixture well and continue to cook, stirring every 30 minutes until cooked.

Garnish with olives and Chinese parsley.

Makes 6 to 8 portions. *(1 portion = 478 calories, 4.1 grams fat, 13% protein, 79% carbohydrates, 8% fat)*

Confetti Congee

Congee, also known as "Cheuk" or "Jook" is a Chinese dish that is a rice porridge. This dish can also be called "Rainbow Congee" because of the colors added to the otherwise plain color of rice. It is surprisingly enjoyable for breakfast. ∞

3 C	Long grain or short grain rice
3	Chinese mushrooms *(dried)*
1 tsp.	Peanut oil
3	Carrots
4-5	Shallots, minced
12 C	Vegetarian chicken-flavored broth
2 Tbsp.	Tamari
2 C	Peas *(fresh)*

CONDIMENTS:

Lettuce, shredded
Green onion
Chinese pickles

Wash rice until water runs clear. Drain and set aside.

Cover dried mushrooms with hot water for approximately 20 minutes. Remove from water and trim stems. Dice mushrooms in 1/4" pieces.

In a large stock pot or wok, heat oil and sauté shallots until transparent. Add mushrooms and carrots and simmer for about 1 minute.

At this point this dish can be cooked on the stove or transferred to a crock pot. See crock pot instructions below.

Stir in rice, broth and tamari, and bring to a boil. Cook for about 2 minutes over high heat, stirring occasionally. Reduce heat to low. Cover and simmer for about an hour. The mixture should be the consistency of porridge.

Garnish with condiments.

To Prepare In Crock Pot:

Transfer to crock pot and add rice, broth, and tamari. Cook for approximately 2 minutes, stirring occasionally. Cover and simmer on low heat for 2 hours or until you reach the consistency desired. Add peas and simmer for 10 minutes more.

Garnish with condiments.

Makes 6 portions. *(1 portion = 421 calories, 3.6 grams fat, 12% protein, 50% carbohydrates, 8% fat)*

Baked Rice With Shiitake Mushrooms

This is another dish that always runs out because of its popularity. It was served at the Governor's mansion during the celebration of the Hawaii Health Program. Besides using it as a staple food, I like to add wild rice as a variation and use it for a special Thanksgiving dish. ೞ

2 C	Brown rice
4 - 5	Shiitake mushrooms *(dried)*
2 pinches	Sea salt *(1 pinch per cup of rice)*
2 Tbsp.	Tamari
3-1/2 C	Water

Rinse brown rice until it rinses clear. Soak mushrooms in 1/4 to 1/2 cup water until soft. Reserve soak water. Slice mushrooms into thin slices.

In oblong baking dish, place the rinsed, drained brown rice, shiitake mushrooms, sea salt and 2 tablespoons of tamari. Mix together so that the mushrooms are evenly distributed throughout the rice. Add 3-1/2 cups of water *(includes the soaking water)*. Cover the baking dish and bake in 350° F. oven for 45 to 60 minutes.

Remove from the oven and allow to sit 10 to 15 minutes. Remove cover and serve.

Makes 4 *(1 cup)* portions. *(1 portion = 357 calories, 2.6 grams fat, 8% protein, 85% carbohydrates, 7% fat)*

*Thai Jasmine Rice**

This is another way of preparing rice that adds another dimension to your main staple or side dish. ೧

2 C	Basmati brown rice
1 stalk	Lemon grass *(use blender)*
1/4 C	Sweet yellow onion, chopped
1/4 C	Golden raisins
3 Tbsp.	Jasmine tea, brewed *(use tea bag)*
1 Tbsp.	Fish sauce
2 Tbsp.	Lime peel, grated fine
2 Tbsp.	Lime juice *(fresh)*,
3 sprigs	Mint *(fresh)*, finely chopped

GARNISH:

Lime wedges
Chinese parsley sprigs
Mint sprigs

Steam basmati brown rice until soft and fluffy.

In a large skillet, combine lemon grass, onion, lime peel, lime juice in jasmine tea and fish sauce and parsley stems. Mix in rice and heat through. Remove from heat and fold in chopped mint and golden raisins.

Place in a serving dish and garnish with lime wedges, mint, and parsley.

Makes 4 *(1-1/2-cup)* portions. *(1 portion = 384 calories, 2.8 grams fat, 8% protein, 85% carbohydrates, 7% fat)*

* From **Dr. Shintani's Eat More, Weigh Less® Cookbook**, pages 57-58

Quinoa Pilaf*

Pronounced "keen-wah," this fluffy, tiny grain was a staple of the Incan civilizations and was actually worshipped by them at one time. It has a rich, nutty flavor and is excellent in pilafs, casseroles, as a cereal, and in a variety of other ways. ∽

1/2 C	Mushrooms, sliced
1/2 C	Onion, finely chopped
2 C	Vegetable broth
1 C	Quinoa, toasted *(see below)*
1/2 C	Celery, chopped into about 1/2" segments
1/2 C	Carrot, shredded
1/3 C	Green bell pepper, finely chopped
1/3 C	Red bell pepper, finely chopped
1/3 C	Yellow bell pepper, finely chopped
dash	Sea salt, to taste

Toasted Quinoa:

Rinse thoroughly under cool running water. Place in a 10" to 12" skillet over medium heat; cook, shaking pan occasionally, until quinoa dries and turns golden brown, about 15 minutes. Pour toasted quinoa from pan and let cool. Makes 1 cup.

Pilaf:

Water-sauté onions and mushrooms in a large *(10" to 12")* skillet over medium heat, until onions are caramelized and mushrooms are golden brown.

To water sauté, simply put a few tablespoons of water in a skillet, let it heat, then add onions and mushrooms. Stir often. If it begins to stick, add a bit more water.

Add broth, quinoa, and all vegetables, bring to a boil, lower heat, cover then simmer until liquid is absorbed, about 15 minutes, stirring often.

Makes 6 portions. *(1 portion = 134 calories, 1.8 grams fat, 17% protein, 72% carbohydrates, 12% fat)*

* *From **Dr. Shintani's Eat More, Weigh Less® Cookbook**, page 69*

Maui Tacos' Black Beans

1 lb.	Black beans, triple washed
	Water, to cover
1/4	Onion, chopped
1 tsp.	Salt
1 Tbsp.	Garlic *(granulated)*

Wash beans thoroughly.

In a large pot, add the beans, onions, salt, garlic, and enough water to cover beans while cooking. Bring to a boil, then turn heat to low. Cook for 4 hours or until beans are tender. Remove from heat. Cool. *Leave black beans whole.*

Makes 5 portions. *(1 portion = 125 calories, 0.5 gram fat, 25% protein, 71% carbohydrates, 4% fat)*

Tuscan Beans

1 Tbsp.	Extra virgin olive oil
6 cloves	Garlic, minced
6	Sage leaves *(fresh)*,
2 cans	Canellini beans *(16 oz.)*, cooked
3 C	Tomatoes with juice, crushed, canned
	Salt, to taste
	Pepper, ground, to taste
1 tsp.	Chinese parsley, chopped

In a large saucepan add oil, garlic, and sage. Cover and cook over medium-high heat for 1 minute.

Add beans, tomatoes, parsley, salt, and pepper, stirring constantly. Reduce heat to medium-low and cover. Simmer 10 minutes, stirring occasionally.

Makes 10 portions. *(1 portion = 121 calories, 1.9 grams fat, 21% protein, 65% carbohydrates, 14% fat)*

Fast And Fantastic Desserts

These recipes are designed for a fast meal at home or in the office, and will each serve one or two people. However, the dishes range from simple and hearty to tasteful and elegant. You could also ask a chef to prepare these desserts to top off a well-planned company dinner for a hundred. To serve more people, simply adjust the ingredients accordingly.

Sweet And Warm

Hot Spiced Apples

1	Apple
8 tsp.	Honey
dusting	Cinnamon, ground fine
dusting	Nutmeg, ground fine

Core apple and cut into wedges, unskinned.

Place honey in a bowl. Put in microwave for 1 minute to heat and thin the honey. Remove and roll apple wedges in honey-mixture. *Be careful, it may be hot!* Place honeyed wedges on microwaveable dish and lightly dust with nutmeg and cinnamon. Cook on high for 5 minutes, or according to the microwave's directions. Serve warm.

Makes 1 portion. *(1 portion = 255 calories, 0.5 gram fat, 0% protein, 98% carbohydrates, 2% fat)*

A's Baked Apples

8 medium Apples
1 C   Apple juice
1 Tbsp.   Cinnamon, ground
1/2 tsp. Nutmeg, ground
16   Apricots *(dried)*

Core apple and slice a small hole in top of apple with a vegetable peeler. Core out seeds, leaving the apple whole. Place apples in a baking dish. Add apple juice, cinnamon, ground nutmeg, and apricots to the baking dish. Spoon some of this liquid into the center of each apple. Cover with tinfoil and bake at 350° F. for 10 minutes.

Remove dish from oven, uncover, and pour more liquid into the center of each apple. Cover again and cook for 20 minutes more.

Remove dish again from oven, uncover, and add liquid to the center of apples. Cook uncovered for 5 minutes. *Apples should be soft, but not mushy.*

Remove apples and put on platter or individual dishes.

Remove apricots from sauce. Chop apricots and add to the center of the apples.

Cook sauce until reduced to 1/2 cup. Pour reduced sauce over apples. If you wish, you may drizzle 1/2 teaspoon of honey over each apple. Sprinkle each apple

with cinnamon and nutmeg or, as an option, with raisins.
Serve warm or cold.

Makes 8 portions. *(1 portion = 125 calories, 0.7 gram fat,
2% protein, 94% carbohydrates, 4% fat)*

Stovetop Malted Pears

Barley malt gives this dish a sweet yet nutty flavor. You may also dust the pears with spices of your choice. Cinnamon and nutmeg especially lend themselves to fruit-based recipes, but you may prefer to experiment with other flavorings. Be careful, though, until you understand the varieties of taste and how they blend together. Recipes may be as sensitive as chemical formulations, and one false move can spoil the entire dish. ❦

1 can	Pear halves *(8 oz.)*, unsweetened and drained, juice reserved
2 Tbsp.	Barley Malt sweetener
	Spices of your choice, ground fine *(e.g., cinnamon, nutmeg, cloves)*

Open a can of sugar-free pear halves, drain, and move to a dish. Then brush them with microwave-heated barley malt *(available at your favorite health food store or specialty food store)*.

Preheat skillet. Put a touch of the pear juice in the skillet *(just enough to keep the malted pears from sticking)*. Add pears and heat. Serve warm.

Makes 2 portions. *(1 portion = 81 calories, 0 gram fat, 1% protein, 99% carbohydrates, 0% fat)*

A's Poached Pears

4 medium	Pears, firm but ripe
1 C	Water
3 sticks	Cinnamon
1 tsp.	Vanilla

SAUCE:

1 C	Cooked poaching sauce
	(See cooking instructions below.)
2 Tbsp.	Honey
1	Banana, mashed
1 tsp.	Cinnamon, ground

Cut pears in half. Core out seeds. Place pears, skin side down, in sauté pan. Add water, cinnamon, and vanilla *(poaching sauce)*. Make sure liquid reaches half way up the sides of the pears. Poach pears on low heat for approximately 5 minutes. Do not allow liquid to evaporate. If needed, add more water. Turn pears over gently and cook for 1 more minute. *Pears should be soft, but not mushy.*

Remove pears on to a plate with skin side up. Reserve the liquid from the poached pears. Heat this liquid and add 2 tablespoons of honey and 1 mashed banana. Reduce this mixture to 1/2 cup.

Pour sauce over pears. Arrange cinnamon sticks over pears. Sprinkle with ground cinnamon.

Makes 8 portions. *(1 portion = 83 calories, 0.4 gram fat, 2% protein, 94% carbohydrates, 4% fat)*

Grilled Banana Crisp

2	Bananas
1 C	Granola cereal *(low fat)*
8 tsp.	Honey
dusting	Cinnamon, ground fine

Peel bananas and slice lengthwise, in half.

Preheat toaster oven to "Grill" setting.

In the meantime, mince some low-fat granola cereal by placing it in a coffee/seed grinder and grinding until finer but still crunchy *(about 5 seconds)*.

Thin honey in a microwave, then brush honey over banana. Roll in the granola. Dust with cinnamon and place banana(s) in toaster oven. Grill until golden brown, turning so the golden tone will reach both sides *(about 3 minutes per side)*. Serve warm.

Makes 2 portions.

Haupia

Islanders have enjoyed this local treat for generations. By reducing the quantity of coconut milk, this recipe keeps the fat to a minimum. ∽

2-1/4 C	Rice Dream®
1/4 C	Maple syrup
1/4 C	Coconut milk
2/3 C	Cornstarch
1/2 tsp.	Coconut extract *(optional)*

Combine 1-1/2 cups Rice Dream® and maple syrup in a saucepan. Bring to a small boil. Add coconut milk.

Mix together the remaining Rice Dream® and cornstarch in another small bowl. Add to mixture in saucepan, together with coconut extract, mixing constantly until thickened and mixture boils.

Pour into square pan. Cool and cover with plastic wrap. Refrigerate and cut into squares when ready to serve.

Makes 12 portions.

Banana-Raisin Cookies

2	Bananas *(ripe)*, mashed
1-1/4 C	Rolled oats
1 C	Whole wheat flour
1/2 tsp.	Baking soda
1/2 tsp.	Baking powder
1 tsp.	Cinnamon
1/2 C	Raisins
1 tsp.	Vanilla
1/2 C	Apple juice or water

Preheat oven to 375° F. Combine all the dry ingredients in a large bowl. Add the remaining ingredients and mix well. *Batter should be a little stiff.*

Drop by teaspoon onto a nonstick cookie sheet and flatten slightly. Bake at 375° F. for 15 minutes. Store in an air-tight container.

Makes 16-18 cookies. *(1 cookie = 81 calories, 0.6 gram fat, 11% protein, 82% carbohydrates, 7% fat)*

Apple Bran Cake

2 C	Whole wheat flour
2 C	Bran
2 tsp.	Egg replacer *(optional)*
1 tsp.	Allspice
1 tsp.	Cinnamon
1/2 tsp.	Cloves, ground
1/2 tsp.	Ginger, powdered
2 tsp.	Baking powder
1 C	Honey
1 C	Apples, peeled and diced
1/2 C	Applesauce
1/2 C	Raisins *(optional)*
1/2 tsp.	Vanilla

Mix dry ingredients together.

Mix moist ingredients together.

Add flour mixture to moist ingredients. Stir gently until well mixed. Turn into a square, nonstick baking pan. Bake at 350° F. for 40 to 50 minutes until cake pulls away from side of pan.

Makes 12 portions *(1 portion = 213 calories, 0.9 gram fat, 8% protein, 89% carbohydrates, 4% fat)*

This may also be made in a muffin tin. Other fruit can be substituted for the apples, such as bananas.

Spice Cake

16 oz.	Tofu *(firm)*, drained
1/2 C	Apple juice concentrate *(frozen)*
1/2 C	Orange juice, freshly squeezed
1 C	Maple syrup
2 tsp.	Vanilla
3 C	Whole wheat pastry flour
2 Tbsp.	Baking powder
2 tsp.	Baking soda
1/2 tsp.	Ginger, ground
1/2 tsp.	Mace, ground
3/4 tsp.	Nutmeg, ground
1/4 tsp.	Allspice, ground
1 C	Raisins
1 Tbsp.	Zest of orange *(grated orange part of the rind)*
1/2 tsp.	Cinnamon *(for topping)*
1 jar	Orange marmalade *(8 oz., fruit sweetened)*
16	Pecan halves
	Canola oil cooking spray

Toast pecan halves to light brown in a 250° F oven for a few minutes. Set aside. *(Watch carefully!)*

Mix all dry ingredients together in a large bowl. Fold in spices.

If you are sensitive to spices, you can cut the spice quantities in half or eliminate some. This will, however, give you a much blander cake.

Blend tofu with apple juice, orange juice, maple syrup, and vanilla.

Fold wet mixture into dry mixture until totally mixed. Pour into cake pan coated by canola oil cooking spray. Bake at 350° F. for about half an hour, or until a toothpick in the middle comes out clean.

Baking time varies according to altitude, so use your judgment depending on where you live.

Makes 16 portions *(1 portion = 195 calories, 3.0 grams fat, 12% protein, 75% carbohydrates, 13% fat)*

Carrot Cake

2 cups	Whole wheat flour
3/4 C	Honey
1-1/4 C	Applesauce
4 tsp.	Egg replacer, well mixed in 8 Tbsp. water
1-1/2 tsp.	Baking soda
2 tsp.	Baking powder
2 tsp.	Cinnamon
1/2 tsp.	Nutmeg
1/2 tsp.	Cloves
1/2 tsp.	Allspice
3 C	Carrots, grated
1 can	Pineapple *(8 oz.)*, crushed and slightly drained
1/2 C	Raisins
1 C	Walnuts, chopped *(optional)*

Mix dry ingredients together *(flour, spices, baking soda, and powder)*. Add honey, applesauce, and mixed egg replacer. Mix well. Add carrots, pineapple, raisins, and nuts. Stir well.

Turn into a nonstick baking pan *(13" x 9" x 2")*. Bake at 350° F. for 1 hour.

Makes 12 portions *(3" x 3" square)* *(1 portion with nuts = 218 calories, 3.5 grams fat, 8% protein, 79% carbohydrates, 14% fat) (1 portion without nuts = 187 calories, 0.5 gram fat, 7% protein, 91% carbohydrates, 3% fat)*

Mango Lychee Spoon Cake

1-1/2 C	Mango juice
16 oz.	Mango, sliced
1 C	Lychee, shelled and pitted
2 tsp.	Lemon zest
1/4 C	Lemon juice
1/4 C	Vanilla Rice Dream®
1 C	Whole wheat pastry flour
1-1/2 tsp.	Baking soda
1/4 tsp.	Salt
	Cooking spray

Preheat oven to 350° F.

Combine juice, fruits, and lemon zest. Set aside.

Mix dry ingredients in a bowl. Add Vanilla Rice Dream® and stir only until moistened.

Spray a 2-quart, round casserole dish with cooking spray. Spread the batter into the casserole dish. Spoon the juice and fruit mixture over the batter.

Place into the oven and bake for about 40 to 45 minutes or until golden brown.

Remove from the oven, cool on a rack, and serve warm.

Makes 8 portions *(1 portion = 149 calories, 0.9 gram fat, 7% protein, 89% carbohydrates, 4% fat)*

Berry Nests

PHYLLO NESTS:

8 oz.   Phyllo dough
1/4 C   Honey
2 Tbsp. Lime or lemon juice
         Canola oil cooking spray

Preheat oven at 325° F. Line muffin cups with liners.

Slice phyllo dough into 1/2" slices. Toss to separate strips. Spray with canola oil cooking spray and toss again.

Arrange in muffin cups and bake for 15 minutes or until light brown.

In the meantime, mix honey and lime or lemon juice together.

Remove from oven and brush with honey/lime mixture. Cool.

BERRY COMPOTE:

4 C   Strawberries, fresh sliced
1 Tbsp. Lemon juice
4 Tbsp. Raspberry fruit spread

Heat fruit spread with lemon juice until spread is melted. Pour over strawberries and stir. Cool.

Top phyllo nests with berry compote just before serving.

Makes 4 portions *(1 portion = 211 calories, 2.8 grams fat, 6% protein, 83% carbohydrates, 11% fat)*

Phyllo Strudel

6 large	Phyllo sheets
2 large	Mangos, peaches *(firm, ripe)*, or apples, peeled, cored, and cut into 1/4" slices
1/2	Lemon, juiced and zest grated
1 Tbsp.	Rum
3 Tbsp.	Honey
1/4 tsp.	Cinnamon, ground
1/4 tsp.	Vanilla extract
1 Tbsp.	Cornstarch
1/4 C	Raisins *(optional)*
1/2 C	Bread crumbs
	Butter-flavored cooking spray

In a medium bowl, mix lemon juice, zest, rum, honey, cinnamon, vanilla, and cornstarch. Add fruit and raisins, if desired. Marinate for 10 to 15 minutes.

Preheat oven to 375° F.

Place a strainer over a small saucepan, and strain fruit. Put fruit back into the bowl and set aside.

Cook marinade over medium heat, stirring constantly until mixture thickens. Cool 2 minutes, then gently stir into fruit. Set aside.

Place 1 phyllo sheet on a work surface. Spray entire surface lightly with cooking spray, then lightly sprinkle with bread crumbs. Repeat process with remaining phyllo sheets, layering them on top of the first.

Place fruit mixture in one line on short side of phyllo sheets, leaving 1" from each side free of any filling, and roll to a firm tube.

Spray tops and side of roll with cooking spray. Score tops into 12 equal sections. *(This will allow you to slice through cleanly after baking.)* Transfer to a baking sheet with seam side down.

Bake for about 25 to 30 minutes or until golden brown. Cool slightly. Slice and serve warm or at room temperature.

Makes 6 portions *(1 portion = 170 calories, 1.5 grams fat, 6% protein, 86% carbohydrates, 8% fat)*

Fast And Frosty

Melon Balls In Wine Syrup

2 C	Honeydew melon chunks, about 2" square, chilled
1 C	Cantaloupe chunks, about 2" square, chilled
4 Tbsp.	Sweet white wine, *(dealcoholized is best, available at most supermarkets and specialty food stores)*
1 Tbsp.	Lemon zest *(fresh)*
1/2 tsp.	Lemon juice *(fresh)*
1 Tbsp.	Cinnamon, ground
2 Tbsp.	Honey
sprigs	Mint *(fresh)*, to garnish

Mix melon balls together, refrigerate.

Make wine syrup by heating honey in saucepan, then adding lemon juice and zest, and finally the white wine. Stir until blended.

Pour over chilled melon mixture and serve in individual frosted parfait dishes, topped with a sprig of mint.

Makes 6 portions. *(1 portion = 62 calories, 0.2 grams fat, 3% protein, 94% carbohydrates, 3% fat)*

To frost a glass, rinse quickly in cold water and place directly into freezer. When you remove it, the glass or dish will have a refreshing frost to help preserve the chill of your cold desserts.

Carob-Dipped Strawberries

3 C   Strawberries *(fresh)*, chilled, scrubbed,
         with tops removed

CAROB DIPPING SAUCE:

4 Tbsp.   Carob powder *(available at health food stores)*
4 Tbsp.   Honey, thick
dusting   Cinnamon *(optional)*
dusting   Cardamon *(optional)*

To make the sauce, heat the honey in a small sauce-pan, add spices *(if you use them)*, then stir in carob powder. Turn off heat and let thicken for a few minutes.

Carob tastes a great deal like chocolate but has virtually no fat, whereas chocolate is an extremely high-fat food and should always be avoided.

Arrange strawberries in a design of your choice on a chilled glass serving dish, with a matching bowl of the carob sauce in the center; or, you may serve individual portions, with accompanying sauce. Chill the strawberries before serving, but chill the sauce only if it's too thin.

Makes 6 portions. *(1 portion = 74 calories, 0.3 gram fat, 3% protein, 94% carbohydrates, 3% fat)*

For a special touch, add 1 tablespoon of creme de cacao liqueur to your sauce.

Jamaican Ice Dream

1/4 C	Coffee, brewed, chilled *(decaf only)*
1 tsp.	Rum extract
1 tsp.	Raisins, plumped, for topping
4 C	Bananas slices, frozen

Soak raisins in water until soft, about 1/2 hour.

Use your food processor to slice frozen bananas *(slicing blade)*, then pour them into a separate mixing bowl and remove the slicing attachment from processor. Put in the S-blade.

Quickly return newly sliced and still frozen bananas to processor bowl *(they'll thaw quickly now)*. Blend until the bananas have the texture of a very rich ice cream *(usually just a few minutes)*. Add coffee and rum extract, then blend until well mixed *(another minute or two)*.

Replace in mixing bowl and put in coldest part of freezer, leave about 5 minutes or until slightly set.

Serve in an ice cream dish or bowl, topped with raisins. You can also add a tablespoon full of raw carob powder, mixed well, to turn it into a mocha treat.

Makes 8 portions. *(1 portion = 107 calories, 0.6 gram fat, 4% protein, 92% carbohydrates, 4% fat)*

*Honey Almond Fruit Cocktail**

1 C	Watermelon
1 C	Honeydew melon
1 C	Apple
1/2 C	Cantaloupe or pineapple chunks
1	Peach or pear
6 Tbsp.	Agar
2 C	Water
1 C	Unsweetened soy milk
3 Tbsp.	Honey
	Almond extract, to taste

Dissolve agar in water, heat. When completely dissolved, add soy milk, honey, and almond extract, to taste. Cool and let set. Cut into small chunks.

Cut watermelon, honeydew melon, apple, cantaloupe, and peach or pear into 1/2" chunks.

Mix agar chunks together with chunks of various fruits for an unusual and colorful fruit cocktail.

Makes 8 portions. *(1 portion = 85 calories, 0.6 gram fat, 7% protein, 87% carbohydrates, 6% fat)*

* From **Dr. Shintani's Eat More, Weigh Less® Cookbook**, page 314

Pineapple Sorbet

2 C   Pineapple *(fresh)*, in chunks without any
           added juice
1-1/2 C   Ice cubes

GARNISH:

sprigs   Mint *(fresh)*
           Maraschino cherries, red

In food processor, use S-blade to mince pineapple, feed in ice cubes and process until frosty.

Remove to glass serving dishes *(frosted if possible)*, and return to freezer for a few minutes. Just before serving, garnish with a cherry and a sprig of mint.

Makes 6 portions. *(1 portion = 26 calories, 0.2 gram fat, 3% protein, 90% carbohydrates, 7% fat)*

Lime-Honey Shave Ice

In some parts of the world, a Shave Ice is known as a Snow Cone. Whatever you call it, this thirst-quenching snack adapts itself admirably to a full-on dessert treat. Try this honey-lime version first, then design some of your own.

2	Limes, halved
2 Tbsp.	Honey
6 C	Ice cubes or shaved ice, if available

Squeeze lime juice into a container, then quickly grate peel into zest and add to juice, reserving 2 teaspoons for garnish. Mix both with honey, set aside in freezer to chill.

If you're starting with ice cubes, use the S-blade in your food processor to turn the ice to shaved ice, adding in the lime-mixture as you go.

Or if you start with shaved ice, pack it densely into tall, frosted glasses, pour over 2 tablespoons of the lime juice mixture. *(Not too much, or it will melt. You must work quickly, so it won't melt.)* Garnish with zest, then return to freezer to set until time to serve.

You may also try a more time-saving variation by freezing grape or other juice into cubes, then "shaving" that ice directly to serve as dessert.

Makes 6 portions. *(1 portion = 28 calories, 0 gram fat, 2% protein, 97% carbohydrates, 1% fat)*

ଛ

Chapter 6
HawaiiDiet™
for the Health
of the World

Planting the Seeds ('*Ano 'Ano*) for World Health

The restoration of healthy diet and lifestyle based on traditional ways and spiritual values is the key to both physical and spiritual health.

I believe that diet is the most important element of physical health. Faith, prayer, and an understanding and practice of the concepts of *lokahi* and *aloha* ("universal love") are the most important elements of spiritual health.

When an individual becomes truly "whole," that is, healthy in all aspects of his or her life, that individual also has the potential to influence all humanity. It is our hope that this book will help inspire more individuals to seek this wholeness. In this way, they may enhance their contribution to the restoration of the health of the community, the nation and the world.

The ultimate state of global health ideally includes world peace. While this may seem an unachievable goal, humanity has proven time and again that what we can believe, we can indeed achieve. Matthew 17:20 tells us:

> "... if you have faith as a mustard seed, you will say to this mountain, 'Move from here to there,' and it will move; and nothing will be impossible for you."

If we have faith — if we believe in world health and world peace — these beliefs can become a reality.

But — and I cannot stress this enough — world health and world peace must begin with the healing of the individuals who make up the world. It can occur only when people begin to heal themselves, and this healing will take place one step, one day, one person at a time. Diet and lifestyle changes are essential, at the individual level, if this is ever to occur.

Return to the Source

As we have seen, the concepts such as *lokahi* and *aloha* derive from the ancient Hawaiian wisdom that is also found in many other cultures. You don't need a college degree to grasp that these are fundamental concepts. Yet they have more healing power than all the technology on earth.

My descriptions of these concepts are necessarily offered from the perspective of a health care professional whose understanding of the Hawaiian culture comes from my work in the community and with my adopted Native Hawaiian family. But I have also studied the Asian medical arts, and learned to my delight that they are rooted in the same essential understanding. Many Hawaiian healers have a deeper understanding of these concepts and may explain them better than I can. Therefore, I encourage any serious student of the medical arts to seek such an expert. Return to the source, in nature and in natural wisdom, so you may gain as much understanding of these concepts as possible. Take them into your heart, just as the ancestors did.

In the end, we will realize that the future of the world depends on the understanding of *lokahi*, the practice of *aloha*, and faith in God. We must come to a realization that it is the Almighty who does the healing, through his laws of nature. Only then will we fully understand that it is sheer vanity and arrogance to think that our high-tech procedures and designer drugs provide anything that resembles health. In an age where bacteria and viruses increasingly resist antibiotics; where AIDS, heart disease, cancer and other devastating diseases are beyond the healing abilities of modern medicine, we must look for new ways, and we must take the responsibility upon ourselves to do what is necessary to heal ourselves and our world.

We are finding new hope in the old ways, in an integration of ancient traditional concepts with modern science and in a renewed faith in God. The HawaiiDiet™ provides a tool with which to begin the process of healing ourselves. Now it is up to us.

ഇ

Suggested Reading

Shintani TT. *Dr. Shintani's Eat More, Weigh Less® Diet*, Halpax Publishing, Honolulu, 1993.

Shintani TT. *Dr. Shintani's Eat More, Weigh Less® Cookbook*, Halpax Publishing, Honolulu, 1995.

Shintani TT and Hughes C. *The Wai'anae Book of Hawaiian Health, The Wai'anae Diet Program Manual*, Waianae Coast Comprehensive Health Center, Waianae, HI, 1993.

Arnot R. *Dr. Bob Arnot's Revolutionary Weight Control Program*, Little, Brown & Co., Boston, 1997.

Harris W. *The Scientific Basis of Vegetarianism*, Hawaii Health Publishers, Honolulu, 1995.

Heidrich R. *A Race for Life*, Hawaii Health Publishers, Honolulu, 1991.

Heidrich R. *A Race for Life Cookbook*, Hawaii Health Publishers, Honolulu, 1993.

Kushi M, et al. *One Peaceful World*, St. Martin's Press, New York, 1987.

Kushi M. *The Cancer Prevention Diet*, St. Martin's Press, New York, 1983.

Lappé FM. *Diet for a Small Planet*, Ballantine Books, New York, 1982.

McDougall J, *A Challenging Second Opinion*, New Century Publishers, Inc., Piscataway, NJ, 1985

McDougall J, et al. *The McDougall Plan for Super Health and Life-long Weight Loss*, New Century Publishers, Inc., Piscataway, NJ, 1983.

Ornish D. *Dr. Dean Ornish's Program for Reversing Heart Disease*, Ballantine Books, New York, 1991.

Robbins J. *Diet for a New America,* Stillpoint, Walpole, NH, 1987.

Turner K. *The Self-Healing Cookbook,* Earthtones Press, Grass Valley, CA, 1989.

ಐ

Bibliography

Foreword

[1] Shintani TT, Hughes CK, Beckham S, O'Connor HK. Obesity and cardiovascular risk intervention through ad libitum feeding of traditional Hawaiian diet. Am J Clin Nutr, 1991;53:1647S-51S.

Chapter 4

[1] Snowdon DA. Animal product consumption and mortality because of all causes combined, coronary heart disease, stroke, diabetes, and cancer in Seventh-day Adventists. Am J Clin Nutr, 1988;48:739-48.

Chapter 5

[1] O'Connor HK, Teixeira RK, Tan M, Beckham S, Shintani TT. *Wai'anae Diet Cookbook 'Elua, Volume II.* Waianae Coast Comprehensive Health Center, Waianae, HI, 1995.

All Chapters

Shintani TT. *Dr. Shintani's Eat More, Weigh Less® Diet*, Halpax Publishing, Honolulu, 1993.

Shintani TT. *Dr. Shintani's Eat More, Weigh Less® Cookbook*, Halpax Publishing, Honolulu, 1995.

Glossary

O'Connor HK, Teixeira RK, Tan M, Beckham S, Shintani TT. *Wai'anae Diet Cookbook 'Elua, Volume II.* Waianae Coast Comprehensive Health Center, Waianae, HI, 1995.

Pukui MK, Elbert SH. *Hawaiian Dictionary*, University of Hawaii Press, Honolulu, 1992.

Pukui MK, Elbert SH, Mookini ET. *Place Names of Hawaii*, Rev. and Enl. Ed., 2nd ed.; University of Hawaii Press, Honolulu, 1989.

Glossary

Aburage: Japanese deep-fried tofu skin that is often used as a "cone" sushi wrap.

Agar Flakes: Also called agar-agar, this is a mineral-rich seaweed processed into a form that can easily substitute for gelatin.

'Ahi: Hawaiian tuna fishes, especially the yellowfin tuna. It is red when raw and turns white after cooking.

Arame: A high-calcium food (like almost all seaweeds), this Japanese seaweed is a "stringy" sea vegetable like hijiki.

Azuki Beans: Tiny, hard red beans from Japan with a faintly sweet flavor. Also mistakenly called "Aduki."

Basmati Rice: This is a rich and aromatic grain from India. It is known as the "King of Rice" and is eaten by India's elite. *Best when eaten in the brown variety.*

Black Bean Paste: Salty fermented beans used in Chinese cooking.

Broke Da Mouth: So onolicious it "broke da mouth" or "broke da mout." See " 'ono" in this glossary.

Buckwheat: This is a plant seed from the buckwheat plant, which is related to rhubarb. The iron and mineral content is especially high, and this food has been a staple in Russia, Eastern Europe, and China for centuries. It may be prepared in a variety of ways, such as breakfast "cereal" *(though is it not technically a cereal grain)*, pilafs, and other tasty treats. Roasted buckwheat is also known as Kasha, and this grain is increasingly popular in health food cereals.

Chapati: An East Indian unleavened flat bread that is much like flour tortillas, and which make an excellent sandwich.

Chicken-Flavored Vegetarian Broth: See "Vegetarian Chicken Seasoning" below.

Cilantro: A parsley also known as Chinese parsley and coriander.

Chop Chae: Stir-fried Korean dish of vegetables and noodles.

Chinese Parsley: Also known as cilantro and coriander.

Chinese Wood Ears Fungus: Dried black Chinese fungus sold in Oriental food sections or Chinatown markets.

Coconut Milk: The inside juice of the coconut seed. Can be bought in canned form. The pulp of the seed is white and eaten raw or shredded and sweetened as found in the grocery store.

Congee: Chinese rice porridge also known as "jook."

Fish Sauce: A thick, brown, salty sauce made from anchovies.

Gandule: Tropical legume used by Puerto Ricans; also known as pigeon peas.

Garbanzo Beans: Also known as chickpeas, these are highly popular in the Middle East. There are many healthy foods derived from Middle East cuisine. These are high in protein, can be mashed into paste with a bit of lemon oil and fresh garlic, and eaten as a dip for pita bread or used as a sandwich filler. They are also sometimes ground into flour.

Ginger Root: A root which adds a spicy flavor to many Oriental dishes; used sliced or grated; found in most grocery stores.

Golden Needles: Chinese dried lily flower sold in Oriental food sections or Chinatown markets.

Haupia: Hawaiian coconut pudding.

Hawaiian Salt: Sea salt *(pa`akai)*. Coarse salt, rock salt. The Native Hawaiians used to have salt farms in which pools with salt water were dried and salt collected. The crust from tide pools is also collected and kept in bags to use.

Hijiki: A high-calcium food which is a stringy Japanese seaweed similar to arame.

Ho'i'o: A Hawaiian native fern that is also known as "fiddle head" fern. Young fronds are eaten raw. The Japanese call this fern "warabi" and use it in cooking.

Hoisin Sauce: A delicious sweet and tangy sauce made from fermented and seasoned yellow beans and red rice. *(Chinese)*

Jai: Known as monk's food, a traditional vegetarian dish served at Chinese New Year.

Jook: Chinese rice porridge that is also known as "congee."

Kalo: Taro, the staff of life, is a main staple of the Native Hawaiian people of past and present. Good taro is a prized food in Hawaii.

Konbu: A broad, thick Japanese seaweed also known as kelp or laminaria that is used both as a high calcium food as well as the basis of soup stock.

Koshi An: Sweetened azuki beans.

Lawalu: A bundle of food , usually fish, which has been wrapped in taro leaves, wrapped again in ti leaves, tied, and steamed in the imu, a Hawaiian underground oven.

Lemon Grass: Introduced to Hawaii, this herb with long green leaves with a sour flavor is used for tea and cooking. The root, which gives off a ginger-like flavor, is also used in cooking. Commonly used in Southeast Asia cooking.

Limu: Hawaiian word for seaweed.

Lipids: A category of substances that are not water soluble including, for example, fats, oils, and cholesterol.

Lomi *(style)*: To rub, press, crush, massage, rub out; to work in and out. *(Hawaiian)*

Long Rice or Cellophane Noodles: Dried, transparent noodles made out of mung bean starch. Cooks quickly.

Lu'au: Cooked taro leaves, usually boiled in water and other ingredients added. A favorite at any Hawaiian party *(Lu'au)*.

Lychee: A delicious fruit with sweet, soft, juicy meat surrounded by a reddish woody shell that needs to be removed before eating the fruit.

Mamaki: A small, native Hawaiian tree whose bark is used to make cloth *(kapa or tapa)* and the leaves are used for tea

Manapua: A Chinese steamed dumpling traditionally filled with meat or sweets. Known in Chinese as Bao or Dim Sum.

Maui Onion: A mild, sweet onion grown on the island of Maui and a favorite in the Islands.

Mirin: A sweet Japanese rice cooking wine.

Miso: A thick, fermented soybean paste product which has a savory flavor often used in soups and sauces.

Mung Beans: These green or yellow beans are highly popular in Asia, where they are used in vegetable dishes or are sprouted and eaten as sprouts.

Musubi: Japanese name for "rice ball."

Namasu: Japanese vinegared vegetable salad.

Namul: Korean dish of slightly cooked vegetables in a sauce of vinegar, soy sauce, and sesame seeds.

Nutritional Yeast: This golden-colored condiment is also sometimes used as a dietary supplement. It has a distinct but pleasant flavor that adapts itself well to a variety of dishes, from nutty to cheesy. It is available in flaked or powdered form in natural food stores and some supermarkets. Don't mistake it for the ordinary form of baking yeast. It's altogether different *(also known as Brewer's yeast)*.

Ogo: The Japanese name for manauwea, a small red seaweed.

Ono (Wahoo): A fish similar to mackerel or tuna with white, delicate, flaky meat.

'Ono: This word is also used to describe food as delicious, tasty, savory; to relish, crave; deliciousness, flavor, savor.

Pansit: Filipino noodles.

Papaya: A very popular pear-shaped fruit with yellow skin when ripe and yellow to sunrise pink flesh inside.

Phyllo: Dough in very thin sheets, becoming very flaky when baked. *(Greek)*

Pita Bread: A flat, round bread that when cut in two, forms two pieces of pocket bread that can be stuffed to make sandwiches.

Poi: Pudding-like substance pounded from cooked taro root; a staple starch of the Hawaiians.

Quinoa: Pronounced "keen-wah," this fluffy tiny grain was a staple of the Incan civilizations, and was actually worshipped by them at one time. It has a rich nutty flavor, and is excellent in pilafs, casseroles, as a cereal and in a variety of other ways.

Rice Milk (Rice Dream®): Milk made by blending rice and water.

Rice Sticks: Dried rice noodles.

Rice Vinegar: Mild Japanese vinegar.

Seitan: A chewy, high-protein food made from boiled or baked wheat gluten mixed with water and seasonings. Seitan has the chewy texture of meat and is used as a meat substitute. Available in natural food stores.

Shave Ice: Ground up ice as in snow cone.

Shiitake Mushroom: A delicious Japanese mushroom, sold in either fresh or dried form. The dried mushroom is easily used by soaking in water for 10 minutes. The soaking water can also be used in the recipe.

Soba: Long, thin buckwheat noodles, used in a variety of Asian salads and soups.

Somen: Smaller Asian noodles, fast-cooking, and made from various grains.

Sushi: A traditional Japanese food based on rice flavored with vinegar. It is usually served with nori seaweed, wrapped around rice and other ingredients.

Soy Milk: Whitish creamy drink is made from soybeans.

Tahini: Sesame butter, used in a variety of foods, including desserts. This is a high-fat food, so use sparingly if at all.

Tamari: Genuine tamari is soy sauce made naturally without wheat as a by-product of miso making. However, it is commonly used as a term simply describing naturally brewed soy sauce.

Taro: A starchy tuber that is a staple of the Hawaiians; also known as *kalo*.

Tarragon: French tarragon is the preferable kind of this spice. Other brands tend to be tasteless, so look for the "French" name on the label.

Tempeh: A whole soybean food that is a good meat substitute. It is fermented, which minimizes its "beany" flavor and gassiness.

Texturized Vegetable Protein (TVP): Usually referred to by the abbreviation of "TVP." A textured soy product made from extruded soy flour. Used for making sauces, it has the texture of ground meat. Available at natural food stores in minced, granule, and chunk form.

Ti Leaves: Also known as *"ki"* in Hawaiian. A woody plant in the lily family. It has good-sized leaves that are smooth, dark green, and long oval shaped. Most Hawaiian families have ti plant growing in their yards because it has many uses such as luau decoration, ceremonial bundles, to wrap food for cooking, to wrap a lei for a gift, to hang on an object for good luck, for lei making, to bless with, etc.

Tofu: Fermented soybean curd.

Tomatillo: A savory Mexican vegetable that resembles a small, firm, green tomato with a unique flavor unlike a regular tomato.

'Uala: Hawaiian word for sweet potatoes.

Umeboshi: A Japanese pickled plum which has a strong tart and salty flavor. In Japan, it is used as a condiment as well as a folk medicine.

Wakame: A tender, leafy Japanese seaweed, high in calcium as are just about all other seaweeds.

Wok: Pan with curved bottom and sides used in Chinese and other Oriental cookery.

Vegan Diet: A diet which eliminates all animal products, such as meat, poultry, fish, eggs and dairy products.

Vegetarian "Chicken" Broth: See "Vegetarian Chicken Seasoning" below.

Vegetarian "Chicken" Seasoning: A powdered product that is made from vegetable products and spices, that has a chicken flavor. It is used for soup bases and gravies.

Wild Rice: This is actually a grain, from the grass family of foods, rather than rice. But it resembles rice and is used in much the same way, and therefore is always referred to as rice. It is highly nutritious, and has a light, subtle taste. Excellent in pilafs, or combined with other types of rice.

80

Recipe Credits

The Recipes in this book were created through the efforts of a number of people and a combination of a number of programs that I have conducted through my private practice and the Hawaii Health Foundation. I would like to thank the following people for their help in producing these recipes.

Carol Devenot, an award-winning Family and Consumer Science teacher, was my chief recipe editor, tester, and advisor. *(She is so talented; she even painted the cover.)*

David McDonald, our logistics officer, tirelessly checked our work and calculations and helped us meet our deadlines.

Lynne Lee, an award-winning Family and Consumer Science teacher, was one of the chief cooking instructors of the Hawaii Health Program Seminars.

Jenny Choy, a Family and Consumer Science teacher, has worked for many years at Kamehameha Schools with Native Hawaiian children and is one of the chief cooking instructors of the Hawaii Health Program Seminars.

Ann Tang, a home cooking expert, contributed some of the recipes and dressings.

Jan Miller, my writer who is also a home cooking expert, contributed a number of recipes, including some of the delicious desserts.

Dick Algire, a local TV celebrity with KITV News 4, allowed me to use his "Lazy Enchilada" recipe from his book *Cook Healthy Fast.*

From the Waianae Coast
Comprehensive Health Center

Sheila Beckham, M.P.H., R.D., was the chief dietitian for the HawaiiDiet™ Study, the Hawaii Health Program, and a member of our recipe committee.

Stephen Bradley, M.D., a remarkable physician who is an orthopedist, family practitioner, and, believe it or not, a certified chef!

Helen Kanawaliwali O'Connor wrote many of the traditional Hawaiian recipes which came from *Wai'anae Diet Cookbook 'Elua, Volume II.*

Rozalyn Kalei'aukai Teixeira wrote many of the traditional Hawaiian recipes. *Wai'anae Diet Cookbook 'Elua, Volume II.*

Mahalo

Alouette's Custom Designed Catering (808-523-1254) deserves credit for some of the delicious salsas and dressings on the program that appear in the book.

Special Thanks

Special Thanks to some of the **Hawaii Regional Cuisine Chefs** who helped with some of our fancier recipes.

Peter Merriman, Chef/Owner of "Merriman's Restaurant" in Kamuela, Hawaii (808-885-6822) and Chef/Partner of "Hula Grill" in Ka'anapali, Maui (808-667-6636) helped us plan the Hawaii Health Program and contributed some exotic recipes to this book.

Mark Ellman, Chef/Owner of "Avalon" in Lahaina, Maui (808-667-5559) and partner in six "Maui Tacos" restaurants on the Big Island of Hawaii, Maui, and Oahu, helped plan the Hawaii Health Program, and contributed a number of recipes including the Maui Tacos selections.

Roy Yamaguchi, Chef/Owner of "Roy's Restaurant" in Honolulu (808-396-7697), Maui, Waikaloa, Poipu, Pebble Beach, Seattle, Japan, Hong Kong, and Guam, generously contributed a signature dish of his and other recipes, and allowed us to adapt them slightly for simplicity's sake.

℘

Shintani's Mass Index of Food
SMI (or "EMI") Table

Food	SMI	Food	SMI
Almonds	0.9	Bread, Wheat*	4.8
Apples	9.4	Blueberries	8.8
Apricots	10.0	Bread, White*	4.6
Apricots, Dried	3.4	Broccoli	10.0
Artichokes	10.0	Brussel Sprouts	10.0
Asparagus	10.0	Buckwheat (ckd)*	7.9
Avocado	3.3	Butter	0.8
Bacon	0.8	Cabbage	10.0
Bagel*	4.2	Cabbage, Chinese	10.0
Bamboo	10.0	Cantaloupe	10.0
Banana	6.4	Carrots	10.0
Barley (ckd)*	5.5	Cashew Nuts	1.0
Bass	2.1	Cauliflower	10.0
Beans	4.6	Celery	10.0
Beans, Garbanzo	5.6	Cheese, Blue	1.5
Beans, Green	10.0	Cheese, Cheddar	1.4
Beans, Kidney	4.6	Cherries	8.7
Beans, Lentils	5.2	Chestnuts	2.8
Beans, Lima	4.9	Chicken, Whole	2.2
Beans, Mung Sprt.	10.0	Chicken, Dark	3.1
Beans, Navy	4.6	Chicken, Fried	2.2
Beef, Chuck	1.4	Chicken, White	3.3
Beef, Corned	1.5	Chocolate Candy	1.0
Beef, Ground	1.9	Coconut Meat	1.6
Beef, Steak	1.2	Collards	10.0
Beets	10.0	Corn	6.5
Blackberries	9.4	Corn Chips	2.0

* SMI numbers have been adjusted upwards to account for increased bulk of this food in the stomach due to absorption of water.

Food	SMI	Food	SMI
Crab Salad	3.8	Loquats	10.0
Crackers, Cheese*	2.3	Lychees	10.0
Cranberries	10.0	Mackerel	2.3
Crab	5.9	Mangos	8.3
Cream Cheese	1.5	Margarine	0.8
Cucumbers	10.0	Mayonnaise	0.8
Donuts	1.3	Melon	10.0
Eggplant	10.0	Millet (ckd)*	6.1
Eggs	3.4	Mushrooms	10.0
Endive	10.0	Mustard Greens	10
Figs	6.8	Nectarines	9.3
French Fries	1.7	Oatmeal	9.9
Garlic	4.1	Oil/Lard	0.6
Ginger	10.0	Okra	10.0
Grapefruit	10.0	Olives	4.7
Grapes	10.0	Onion, Green	10.0
Ham	2.1	Onions	10.0
Ham Sandwich	1.6	Oranges	10.0
Hamb, 1/4 lb w ch	2.1	Pasta	4.1
Hamburger, 1/4 lb	2.2	Pastry(Danish)	1.5
Hard Candy	1.4	Peaches	10.0
Honey	1.8	Peanut Butter	0.9
Kale	10.0	Peanuts	0.9
Kumquats	10.0	Pears	9.0
Lamb, Leg	2.9	Peas	6.5
Lamb, Loin Chop	2.2	Peppers, Chili	10.0
Lemon	10.0	Persimmons	5.3
Lentils	5.2	Pineapples	10.0
Lettuce	10.0	Pistachio Nuts	0.9
Lobster	5.8	Plum	9.1
Loganberries	8.8	Poi	9.1

* SMI numbers have been adjusted upwards to account for increased bulk of this food in the stomach due to absorption of water.

Food	SMI	Food	SMI
Pork	2.1	Tofu	7.6
Pork, Loin	2.3	Tomato	10.0
Potato	9.6	Tomato Paste	6.5
Potato Chips	2.0	Tuna in Water	4.3
Pretzels*	3.1	Tuna Sandwich	2.1
Prunes	6.8	Tuna, in Oil	1.9
Pumpkin	10.0	Turkey	2.1
Radish	10.0	Turkey Sandwich	2.1
Raisins	1.8	Turnip	10.0
Raspberry	7.5	Veal	3.4
Rice, Brown*	6.1	Walnut	0.9
Rice, White	5.0	Watercress	10.0
Saltine Crackers*	1.2	Watermelon	10.0
Scallop	4.9	Whole Wht Bread*	4.7
Seaweed(konbu)	10.0	Yam	6.3
Seaweed(wakame)	10.0	Zucchini	10.0
Sesame	0.9		
Shrimp	4.8		
Shrimp, Fried	2.3		
Soybean	4.2		
Soybean, Sprouts	10.0		
Spaghetti	4.8		
Spinach	10.0		
Squash	10.0		
Strawberries	10.0		
Sturgeon	3.4		
Sugar	1.5		
Sunflower Seeds	1.0		
Sweet Potato	5.4		
Tangerines	10.0		

* SMI numbers have been adjusted upwards to account for increased bulk of this food in the stomach due to absorption of water.